LIMINAL

Liminal

This book is set in the typeface *Myriad Pro* designed by Robert Slimbach.

Paperback ISBN: 978-1-967262-38-0

A Publication of *Tall Pine Books*
PO Box 42 Warsaw | Indiana 46581
www.tallpinebooks.com

| 1 25 25 20 16 02 |

Published in the United States of America

LIMINAL

THE DELICATE SPACE BETWEEN BREATHS

NEIL BROERE

In Liminal, Neil writes with the poetic precision of a prophet and the compassion of a shepherd companion on the pilgrimage of faith. If you've known seasons in the "hallway" between what was and what will be, then this book will serve as a field guide for navigating transitions well. I found myself "cut" and exposed, only to be comforted and encouraged as I worked through the pages of this book while reflecting on the pages of my life story. I cannot recommend Liminal enough to those who want to "crown" Jesus as King, no matter what season you find yourself in.

–Chad Bohi

Everyone will face transition at some point in their life. Whether you have been there, know it will come, or are in the midst of it now, Liminal is for you. Written from the tender place of devotion to God and building friendship with Him in the trenches of life, Neil shares both powerful revelation and practical instruction from the scriptures and his own life experience that is certain to be a breath of fresh air for those who desire to find satisfaction in God that frees their heart to anchor deeply into the sovereignty of God. Liminal is a book that will help strengthen your confidence in a God that can be trusted. This one deserves a read, and regular rereading, to benefit from the treasure trove that Neil has so beautifully offered to us.

–Michael Dow

This book is essential for every believer who is longing for the Lord to "lift the fog." Part of me wishes, similar to car insurance, that this book would be "required reading" for every believer in Christ! Your "Liminal" time could be now or sometime in the near future, but whenever it is, you can't afford "not" to read this book. This book could not have been written at a more perfect time for my family.

–Paul LaRue

CONTENTS

SECTION III: Open Doors

Liminal (lim - i - nəl) *adj.* **1** Between. **2** Belonging to two different places, states, etc. **3** Of, relating to, or being in an intermediate state, phase, or condition. **4** A metaphorical threshold—as in "the liminal zone between sleep and wakefulness." See synonyms under TRANSITION, THRESHOLD, IN-BETWEEN.

FOREWORD

> "Waiting is not the absence of God's activity; it is often the very place where His most necessary work is taking place." — Neil Broere

Rightly grasping the powerful premise of this book can be the difference between life and death for you. Although that may sound a bit dramatic, I believe with all of my heart that it is true. After reading this manuscript, I've come to the conclusion that every liminal moment that we face holds the potential for us either to experience the resurrection power of the Lord or, sadly, to experience His disappointment due to our selfishness.

If you're anything like I am, the word liminal is not a word that has been in your daily vocabulary. Yet, liminal is a reality with which all of us are faced on a daily basis. In this book, LIMINAL: The Delicate Space Between Breaths, my dear friend Neil Broere has done a masterful job in explaining how liminal seasons are ultimate seasons that will end up shaping and defining our entire life while here on earth.

Whether you consider the pages of Biblical history or open any modern day history book, you'll find that destinies have hung in the balance with each liminal moment faced. Sadly, one such destiny of the newly appointed (and anointed!) King Saul was forfeited when he gave in to his human instinct to react in a way to save his reputation. As in most liminal moments, life and death were in the balance. And, although in the eyes of man he may have 'succeeded,' in the eyes of the Lord, he failed miserably.

> "You have acted foolishly; you have not kept the commandment of the LORD your God, which He commanded you, for now the LORD would have established your kingdom over Israel forever. But now your kingdom shall not endure. The LORD has sought out for Himself a man after His own heart, and the LORD has appointed him as ruler over His people, because you have not kept what the LORD commanded you." (1 Sam 13:13-14)

In less than one full week as king, Saul forfeited his entire God-ordained destiny (where the Lord would have established his kingdom over Israel forever), and chose rather to act on his own behalf, trying to save his reputation as king before men who were fleeing in fear.

Sadly, this ill-advised, temporary, liminal-moment decision lives on eternally through the canon of scripture as how not to respond when your season of waiting seems to be producing a situation that may eventuate into one's failure.

It's no small thing to consider that each choice we make today will have a profound effect, not only on our future, but also on the future destinies of our children and grandchildren. Because the Lord thinks generationally, He's not only concerned about your destiny, but also about the destinies of the generations that will live on long after you take your last breath on this earth.

I've had the joy of knowing Neil and his beautiful family for over 15 years. I have had the privilege of being an eyewitness to some of Neil's defining liminal moments. And, it is those moments that have molded him into the perfect position to author this book. As a faithful husband and loving father, he has shepherded his family through some very challenging moments and seasons. And, although he would be the first to admit he didn't do everything perfectly, I am one that can attest to the fact that if there was a "liminal misstep" along the way, it was accompanied by a humility in Neil that is producing fruit that has remained evident to this day.

LIMINAL will help you navigate through each challenging season you might encounter. In this masterpiece, Neil brilliantly unpacks the scriptures that will both challenge you as well as encourage you. One needs only to look at each of the chapter titles in this manuscript to realize that this book was not written haphazardly, but rather through life experience.

Providentially, we don't have the luxury of going back and changing the choices we made decades ago. But, we do have the luxury of positively affecting our future by the choices we make today. And those choices will not only affect us, but they will also make a difference on the generations that will come after us. That is why I believe that if you rightly understand and value the points Neil makes in this book about every liminal moment, it can be the difference between life and death for you!

Scott Volk
Together For Israel
Founder

INTRODUCTION

THE PAUSE THAT CHANGED EVERYTHING

In the first week of January 1066, the King of England died.

Edward the Confessor had ruled for nearly twenty-four years, a relatively long reign in a time when kings usually died young. It was a season marked by an unusual level of national stability. Edward had waged no wars. He had no bitter enemies. There were no peasant revolts or political purges. Under his leadership, the kingdom experienced something extremely rare in medieval Europe: a sustained period of internal peace.

But Edward had one significant liability: he had no heir.

For a medieval monarch, that wasn't just an inconsequential footnote. It was a generational time bomb.

Less than twenty-four hours after the death of King Edward the Confessor, Harold Godwinson, an influential noble and military leader, was crowned king.

The transition was fast. Functional. Hurried.

It was a strategic choice made by the King's Council to signal continuity. The coronation was swift because those in control were certain it had to be. The longer the crown sat vacant, the more room there would be for other claims.

And there were, most definitely, other claims.

King Edward's death and the hasty transition of Harold Godwinson to the throne were the beginning of one of the most violent and transformational years in English history.

Three men would claim the throne that year. Two would die for it. And by the end of this pivotal transition, England would never be the same.

While Harold Godwinson believed he was the rightful heir to the throne, *another* man, William, Duke of Normandy, believed *he* had been promised the throne years earlier. He claimed that the previous king of England had traveled to Normandy, modern-day France, and sworn a sacred oath on a box of bones pledging to give *him* the throne. Whether that happened is disputed.

But what's clear is that William saw Harold's coronation not just as a hostile takeover, but a breach of honor... outright sin.

The *other* claim to the throne came from the north.

Harald Hardrada, King of Norway, argued that an ancient agreement between earlier kings of England and Scandinavia entitled *him* to the throne.

What followed was a sequence of invasions almost without parallel in European history: three major military campaigns in less than three months.

In September, Hardrada sailed from Norway and launched his attack. Harold Godwinson, the newly crowned king of England, marched his army north, over 180 miles in four days, an almost impossible pace given the terrain and period. At the Battle of Stamford Bridge, King Harold defeated the Norwegians in what was, by all accounts, a decisive and brutal defense of his throne. It should have been a triumphant beginning to his reign.

But even before the dust settled from the Battle of Stamford Bridge, William, Duke of Normandy, was landing his ships in the southern part of the country. The English forces, already exhausted from their victory in the north, had to march again, this time in the opposite direction.

They made their stand at the Battle of Hastings. The brave Englishmen fought all day to defend their new king. But near nightfall, King Harold was struck down with an arrow through his eye.

On Christmas Day, 1066, William the Conqueror was crowned King of England.

The ripple effect of this transitional year was enormous. They aways are.

William brought with him a new language, a new legal system, and a new philosophy of rule. He redistributed English land to his Norman supporters, displacing almost the entire Anglo-Saxon aristocracy. He introduced French as the language of the royal court and administration, which over the next few centuries would permanently alter the English language.

What began with the death of a king and an expedited transition ended with an entirely new England. To this day, the royal family isn't descended from the line of Edward the Confessor. They are descended from William the Conqueror. England after 1066 was not simply under new management. It was a fundamentally different nation.

All because of what happened in the delicate space between what was and what would be.

This story begs the question: Why are transitions so pivotal? Why is the space between where you were and where you're going so consequential?

Is it true that what happens in the in-between determines everything that happens next?

I believe so.

Like the people of England in 1066, unaware life would never be the same for them, or their descendants, there's a vulnerability that marks those in transition.

Vulnerable because the soul is exposed.

Transition strips away the scaffolding of routine, leaving the soul marooned in the middle; like a bridge under tension, creaking under the weight of those passing through. The weakness isn't because of the weight it bears, but in the fact that it's suspended between two points.

Like a son of Adam pinned between nail points, naked and exposed. The liminal space doesn't just hold us; it strips us. It stretches us across the gap between what was and what isn't yet, laying bare everything we work so hard to keep hidden. We're left hanging, run through by the process, arms stretched wide, heart unmasked, held in tension between Judas's kiss and the empty grave.

We're no longer in control in the liminal space. A higher Authority now occupies that throne.

And it's not just nations and crowns that sway in the liminal space. Scripture is full of delicate, in-between moments:

> Eve stood between temptation and obedience.
> Abraham stood between promise and fulfillment.
> King Saul stood between insecurity and surrender.
> Peter stood between denial and restoration.

Every one of them faced the same question: *what do I do when I don't know what to do next?*

And every one of them shows us how costly it can be to crown the wrong thing in the waiting.

While transition often feels like a battleground, it's also a garden. And some of God's most significant work happens beneath the surface of the liminal space; quietly, out of sight, beyond explanation.

It brings to mind a story from a place far from 11th-century England, one that speaks, in its own way, to the hidden work God does in the in-between.

The Midnight Gardener

In Tokyo, there's a man known as the "midnight gardener." No one knows his real name. He's only seen between 2 and 4 a.m., tending to a narrow strip of dirt beside a highway on-ramp. He plants flowers, pulls weeds, and silently waters his midnight garden by the road.

No one asked the man to do this. He's never been paid for his work. But commuters have noticed the splash of green in the sea of gray.

One day, a sign appeared in the garden:

"Don't despise the place between here and there. Something beautiful is growing."

It's an odd message for a highway on-ramp. Most never even notice that strip of ground, let alone believe anything of value could grow there.

But that's the point. And the midnight gardener's sign became an invitation to acknowledge the beauty of a space most people rush through.

The overlooked space between here and there, what we are calling the *liminal* space, is a lot like that highway on-ramp. It's what you pass *on your way* to where you're going. It appears painfully insignificant. Hardly a place at all. And only *then* because it connects you to your destination. Other than that, the place of transition is usually disregarded.

But God does His best work in unseen places.

Like Pharaoh's prison, where Joseph remained faithful when no one was watching.

Like the fields of Bethlehem, where a shepherd boy learned the heart of a king.

Like the Judean wilderness, where the Baptizer discovered his voice preaching to the wind.

Like the Nazarene village, where a Savior was raised, unnoticed by the world He came to save.

And just like the midnight gardener, God works in our seasons of transition with quiet faithfulness, pulling, pruning, planting, and watering when no one else is watching. We may not see the purpose. We may not even realize He's there. But beneath the surface, something beautiful is growing.

The space between here and there is sacred ground. It's a consecrated soil where roots sink deep. Where beauty quietly breaks through concrete. There's a holiness about the in-between that asks us to remove our shoes as we pass through.

But passing through transition isn't tidy. And this is where the metaphor of the on-ramp begins to break down. The space between seasons is rarely straightforward. And "painfully insignificant" it most certainly is *not*. It's more like a gauntlet of closed doors. The one behind you has shut. The one ahead hasn't opened yet. You're left standing in the middle...waiting.

It's not a garden anymore, it's a hallway. The forgotten space between rooms, useful only because it leads somewhere else. No one celebrates the hallway. They just want out of it.

We don't talk much about that space. There are no holidays for it (would Liminal Space Day be a gift-giving holiday?). No titles. No ceremonies. It is, by definition, simply the forgotten time between things we *do* remember. We're conditioned to measure our lives by the defining moments that easily stand out: The marriage. The diagnosis. The birth. The accident. The move. The breakthrough.

But what about everything in between?

I would submit that the most consequential moments in history aren't defined by the triumphs or tragedies. It's the pause between the two that determines which king is on the throne.

The obscurity of that pause is stunning. Like breathing, you never notice it until you have to. And once you have to notice something like breathing, it's all you can think about.

Consider the pause at the end of your next exhale. Now imagine not knowing when the next breath would come. That's the delicate, vital, hardly-even-a-moment-until-it-becomes-the-only-moment-that-matters pause of the liminal space. A moment too thin for words, but too real to deny.

Most of the time, transitioning between inhale and exhale is easy. We do it 22,000 times a day without batting an eye. But transitioning from one season to another? Now that's a different animal.

But why?

Why would most of us rather stay in the same spot the rest of our lives than endure the in-between, even when the hallway of the in-between leads to God's higher purposes?

One reason: fear.

We're afraid of getting it wrong.

No one's afraid of on-ramps. They only go in one direction. But the hallway of transition presents an endless possibility of *what-ifs*. And in that ambiguity, fear tries to push us into one of two ditches:

- The *paralyzed* freeze. Like deer in headlights, we do nothing. We stall. We stay longer than we're meant to, refusing to move until the path is foolproof.
- The *trigger-happy* jump. We crown the first door that opens, not asking if it's from God, only if it's open.

Both responses short-circuit the deeper work God intends to do in us during the in-between.

But what if the liminal space is actually a gift?

What if the pause is God's way of forming something necessary in us *before* He releases us into the next season?

Could the in-between be God's way of protecting us from being crushed under the weight of answered prayers we don't *yet* have the grace, or character, to carry?

I know the liminal space. I've watched as one season ends before the next one begins. I know what it's like to pray for open doors and only hear the locking of the one behind me. I've felt the allure of moving ahead in my own strength, of attributing something to "God's will" just because it advertised itself as the quickest way to get into it.

I know the temptation to birth Ishmael because Isaac is just taking too long.

But I've also learned to see the liminal space the way God intends for us to see it.

Not as abandonment.

Not as wasted time.

And certainly not as punishment.

I've come to see it as the incubator for all that's needed in the next season. The pause is purposeful. God's orchestrated transitions aren't just footnotes to the larger story, they *are* the story. It's in the delicate space between breaths that the heart adjusts to a new rhythm. It's where faith learns how to breathe without the oxygen of proof.

In the liminal, identity gets untangled from assignment, and hope detaches from outcome.

Or to put it more bluntly, the liminal space is essential if we're ever going to grow up.

I don't know what season you're navigating right now. Odds are you're either in the middle of transition or about to hear the unmistakable 'click' of a door closing behind you.

Go ahead, rattle the handle.

Yup. It's locked.

Your previous season is over, as over as King Edward's reign. What happens next will shape the language you speak the rest of your life.

The hallway you're standing in is not neutral.
Like a vacant throne, it attracts ambition. It amplifies survival instincts. But if you let Him, God will lead you through the transition, and guard you from lesser kings eager to fill the vacuum of the in-between.

If you're trying to make sense of a closed door that you thought would stay open…

If you're holding a promise that hasn't yet come to pass…

If you feel stuck between seasons…

…then hear this: God is in the liminal space. He meets His people there, again and again.

He did it for Joseph.

He did it for David.

He did it for the John the Baptist.

He's done it for me.

And He'll do it for you.

The delicate space between breaths belongs to God.

We began our journey with a story from over a thousand years ago, a moment of hasty transition so monumental it reshaped the world. As we move forward together, we'll hear other tales of transition to help shed light on what can otherwise feel like a dark and confusing hallway. Think of them as portraits hung on the walls of the in-between, reminders that others have walked these halls and found God here.

Our voyage unfolds in three movements:

> The closed door.
> The hallway.
> The open door.

Between each, we'll pause for a "threshold reflection"; a moment to slow down, breathe, and acknowledge the space we're in. By doing this, we mirror the pace of real life in transition: slower than we want, deeper than we expect, and far more sacred than we imagine.

Without further ado, let's find our seats in the liminal space.

SECTION I

CLOSED DOORS

CHAPTER 1

DISAPPOINTMENT & UNMET EXPECTATIONS

"Unmet expectations are where false messiahs are born."

-Unknown

John the Baptist was a steel-spined prophetic voice. Among those born of women, there was none greater than John.

John was the wild one, the voice in the wilderness, the prophet who saw heaven open and the Spirit descend like a dove. He was the shining lamp all of Israel rejoiced in. He was the one preparing the way. He had pointed at Jesus with fire in his bones and shouted, *"Behold, the Lamb of God who takes away the sin of the world."*

John knew who Jesus was.

But then the door closed on his season of forerunning... abruptly, with the cold finality of a prison gate.

One day John was waist-deep in the Jordan, multitudes pressing in to be baptized. The next, he was swallowed up in isolation, the roaring thunder of his voice snuffed out by the solitude of a jail cell. His ministry, the calling that had consumed his life, was suddenly over.

This wasn't how it was supposed to go. The Messiah was supposed to bring justice. Free the oppressed. Tear down the wicked.

Where was the fire from heaven? Where was the axe laid at the root of the tree? John had said those words himself... and now he sat shackled behind bars, waiting for a deliverance that wouldn't come.

Somehow, John was able to get a message to his Cousin. A question wrapped in unmet expectations:

> "Are You the Coming One, or do we *look for another*?"[1]

Look for another? How could someone like John, who had such clarity on what God was doing, now ask such a question?

There's only one reason: because the reality John was living in didn't match the expectation he was holding onto. He still believed in the Coming One, he just didn't expect Him to come like *this*.

---

1. Matthew 11:3

John expected Jesus to storm the palace.
Instead, Jesus quietly healed the blind and preached to the poor.

John expected a political revolution. Jesus brought a kingdom that spreads like leaven.

And so the moment Jesus got word of John's imprisonment, He took off like a speeding bullet to break him out and launch the much anticipated revolution against the tyranny of Caesar.

Not quite.

That's comic-book Jesus. Real Jesus sent John a simple blessing:

> *"Blessed is he who is not offended because of Me."*[2]

In other words: *Blessed is the one who doesn't fall away when I don't meet their expectations.*

Let that settle for a moment…like leaven.

Jesus doesn't correct John's theology. He doesn't scold him for doubting. But He does offer a warning:

> Don't let your confusion create a version of Me that isn't true.
> Don't trade the real Messiah for the one you were expecting.
> Don't let your questions redefine reality.

---

2. Matthew 11:6

In other words: *John, don't start looking for another just because the door closed.*

This is the potential breaking point between what was and what's to come, when your story pauses long enough for you to wonder whether its over…or just intermission.

It's not like transition sends a save-the-date letter. There's no countdown clock letting you know how much longer your season will last. One minute, life is moving forward; the next…thud. The door of that season shuts, and everything you thought would happen is gone.

You're left standing there, holding a suitcase full of unmet expectations, unsure what to do next.

It's disorienting when the momentum of plans, ideas, and expectations slams to a halt. And like John, the confusion of the closed door can tempt us to start scanning the horizon for a replacement. Left unchecked, unmet expectations become a chisel that slowly reshapes faith into something unrecognizable.

But while the season may have changed, Jesus hasn't.

Yet this is where many stumble…when the Jesus standing in front of them doesn't look like the Jesus they were expecting. It happened to John in prison, and it happened to an entire town in Mark's Gospel.

When Jesus Can't Be Himself

Mark records a sobering moment when Jesus returned to His hometown, Nazareth. Like John the Baptist, these were people who *knew* Jesus, at least they thought they did. They'd watched Him grow up. They played alongside Him. In their minds, they had Jesus all figured out.

So when He returned all grown up and began to teach in their synagogue, they were astonished,

> "What's this wisdom that has been given Him? What are these remarkable miracles He is performing?"[3]

The Man in front of them didn't match the boy they remembered. But even though the season had changed for the people of Nazareth, Jesus was still the same. And rather than allowing the Rabbi to redefine who He had always been, they held on to their expectation of who He should be based on their experience of Him,

> "Wait a minute, isn't this the carpenter? Isn't this *Mary's* son?"

Those words were laced with scandal.

By "Mary's son," they weren't thinking family tree; they meant *that* Mary, the one who had her first baby not enough months after she got married.

> "And they were offended at Him."[4]

---

3. Mark 6:2
4. Mark 6:3

To them, Jesus was the Son of Mary, not the Son of God. He was the woodworker with the birthday that didn't add up. Nazareth was simultaneously clinging to their expectation of who the Messiah was supposed to be, a king and liberator, and refusing to see anything in Jesus other than the dusty kid from down the road who built their dining table.

And they were *offended* at Him.

The Trap of Offense

This word we translate as "offended" is rich. The Greek word is *skandalízō*. It's where we get our word "scandal" from. The root means "to jump up and snap shut." In its original sense, it described a spring-loaded piece of wood holding open a trap for animals. When triggered, the trap would snap shut, catching its prey.

In Scripture, *skandalízō* is used metaphorically for a stumbling block, something that causes a person to trip and fall. It's a trap, often sprung through misunderstanding or false expectation.

The related noun, *skandalon*, is used throughout the New Testament to describe the offense people took toward Jesus. For example:

- The disciples took offense when Jesus spoke of His sufferings (Matthew 26:31).
- Peter rebuked Jesus when He spoke of the cross: "Never, Lord!" (Matthew 16:22).

- The multitudes were offended at the suggestion that Jesus's body and blood were true food and drink. (John 6:53-56)[5]

Do you see the pattern? In every case, offense came because Jesus didn't fit someone's idea of who the Messiah should be.

And in His hometown, Jesus became a *trap* to the people who knew Him the longest; not because He set one, but because He refused to conform to their expectations. They stumbled because Jesus refused to shrink down to the level of their assumptions.

And the consequence?

> "He could do no mighty works there except heal a few sick people."[6]

Their unbelief about who He was kept Him from being Himself. Their offense reduced the One who holds the world by the power of His word to a handful of healings. Not because His power diminished, but because their *faith* did.

> "And He marveled at their unbelief."[7]

---

5. To be clear, Jesus is not the one setting the trap. He is the stone in Zion over which many will stumble (Romans 9:33). It's the darkness in which many walk that causes them to stumble, not the Stone. The lies believed about who He is blind the world to the truth that Jesus can be trusted, followed, and ultimately be the rock they can build their lives on.
6. Mark 6:5
7. Mark 6:6

They had faith in their *idea* of the Messiah, but not in the Messiah who stood in front of them. And at the end of the day, faith in a false expectation isn't really faith at all.

From Expectation to Hope

When expectation stubs its toe on the rock of reality—when doors close, seasons shift, and what we thought *should* happen doesn't—we're tempted to do what the people of Nazareth did: reduce God to something small. We speak of Him based on what *didn't* happen, rather than what He says *will.*

Why didn't You keep me from getting fired.

Why didn't You make the ministry grow faster.

Why didn't You stop the foreclosure.

Why didn't You…

We all have our own ideas of how things should go in the season God has us in. But God isn't bound to our expectations. And if we're not careful, our disappointment when a season ends before someone asks for our permission can harden into offense. We start to redefine God through the lens of our situation rather than letting Him reveal Himself *through* it. When disappointment becomes our teacher, it will always teach us the wrong lesson. We become disillusioned because God didn't follow our script. But feelings aren't prophets. They don't get the final word. God does. And if we let disappointment define who He is, we end up serving a reflection of our pain instead of the revelation of His nature. God doesn't explain Himself; He reveals Himself. And His revelation rarely comes wrapped in what we expected.

Consider this: Jesus is always with us, but He is not always revealed. He may be in the room, but offense can keep Him hidden. Like Nazareth, unbelief shaped by unmet expectations can hamstring His work in our lives, not because He's less powerful, but because He's not going to force His way into a heart that's closed off, waiting to see it before it believes it.

The antidote? Shift from living with *expectation* to living with *hope*.

You ask, "what's the difference?"

Expectation believes God will do something based on how *we* want the situation to turn out.

Hope believes that whatever God does is good, based on the assurance that He is nothing but loving towards His people.

> "The hope of the righteous is gladness, but the expectation of the wicked perishes."[8]

Expectation is based on what we want to happen.

Hope is based on who God is.

When expectations aren't met, disappointment follows.

---

8. Proverbs 10:28

Hope, however, *never* disappoints.[9]

Hope stares at a closed door and trusts that whatever comes next is better than what came before. Hope is built on the foundation of love; love *for* God and love *from* God,

> "Love bears all things, believes all things, hopes all things, endures all things."[10]

All things. Including the closed door you now find yourself staring at.

If we can face our closed doors with hope instead of disappointment, refusing to let unmet expectations redefine who God is, then we can receive all God intends to do in the liminal space.

> "Hope *completely* on the grace to be brought to you at the revelation of Jesus Christ."[11]

But before we rush ahead, we need to see just how fragile transition can be. Scripture gives us another scene, one that pulls back the curtain on how easily offense can creep in when God speaks or acts in ways we never saw coming.

"Does This Offend You?"

There's a story in John 6 that you won't find on coffee mugs or inspirational posters. Jesus, surrounded by

---

9. See Romans 5:5
10. 1 Corinthians 13:7
11. 1 Peter 1:13

multitudes of followers, is leading them to the edge of a massive transition: out of the familiarity of the old covenant and into the mystery of the new. He gives what may be His most difficult teaching yet:

> "Whoever eats My flesh and drinks My blood has eternal life."[12]

The response from the crowd is exactly what you'd expect: *Nope. I'm out.*

But put yourself in that moment. You haven't read the Passover discourse of John 13-17. You haven't heard, "This is My body broken for you," or "This is the new covenant in My blood." All you've heard is the Man you've watched heal the sick and cast out demons tell you to eat His flesh and drink His blood.

You're not thinking Eucharist.
You're thinking heresy.

You're thinking of the words of Moses, the very law of God that explicitly forbids drinking blood because "the life is in the blood."[13] You're thinking this sounds less like the blessed and holy worship of YHWH and more like something whispered in the darkened temples of pagan gods.

> "Does this offend you?"

Yes, it most certainly does, Jesus. And not just a little.

---

12. John 6:54
13. Leviticus 17:11

Unbelievably, Jesus doesn't walk it back. He doesn't soften the blow, explain the metaphor, or offer theological clarity. He just leaves the statement hanging there, like a door half-open to a room no one's sure they want to enter.

One by one, they turn and leave. The crowd that had pressed in now pulls away. Even the disciples begin to shift uneasily.

Then Jesus turns to the Twelve and asks a question that still echoes in the hearts of all who walk through a disorienting season of transition:

> "Do you want to go away, too?"[14]

What a moment. You can almost hear the awkward silence settle in; the shifting of weight, the uncomfortable clearing of throats, the distant crash of waves cutting through the question of who will be brave enough to speak first.

Twelve men are suddenly aware they're free to leave… just slip back into the anonymity of the crowd, go home and explain away these last few months as a passionate mistake.

But staying means embracing a road that was narrowing with every step, a road that had suddenly taken a hard left when they all expected the Messiah to keep things straight.

---

14. John 6:67

The choice was theirs. No pressure. No manipulation. Just an invitation to stay even when you don't understand. To trust even when you're offended.

Are you so offended by what I've said that you would abandon all we've done because you're unwilling to embrace the confusion?

Finally, one of them speaks up. It's Peter, responding with what might be one of the most courageous confessions in all of Scripture:

> "Lord, to whom shall we go? You have the words of eternal life."[15]

I don't think we appreciate the courage of those words. Jesus had just said something that seemed to contradict the very law God gave to His people. For Peter, it wasn't only personal, it was culturally scandalous. Seemingly heretical. And yet…Peter had seen too much to turn away.

This is what offend-able faith looks like.

Not blind understanding.

Not false expectations.

Just a rugged trust that says: *"Lord, I may not understand what You said, or why You said it, but I trust You. I've heard too much life in Your voice to leave now."*

15. John 6:68

What about you? Does Jesus acting like Himself offend you? Does His truth cut across the grain of everything you think you know? Does Jesus allowing the door to close seem acceptable to you?

Some of the deepest faith you will ever express won't come in your moments of clarity, but in the moments of confusion.

When God doesn't explain Himself…or the door He allowed to close.

When His silence makes you question everything, and still…you stay.

Seeing Him Through the Confusion

What we believe about Jesus when a season comes to an end will either forge Christ-like character in us or shut our hearts down entirely. When the door slams shut and the light from the last season fades, will you worship your idea of what *should* have been, or will you still recognize Him through the confusion?

Will you lay your expectations on the altar of God's will and say, *"Even when I don't understand, I trust that You are good"*?

Because while God can open doors that no man will close, we still have the power, through unbelief, to hamstring Him from being God in those moments when we desperately need Him to be Himself.

Closed doors are hard enough. But holding on to unmet expectations can make them unbearable. That's where offense lies in wait.

But if you can trust Jesus, not only when He acts like what you expect, but when He simply acts like Himself, the closed door becomes something else entirely: an opportunity to grow into the kind of person who can carry what comes next.

CHAPTER 2

WHEN GOD CLOSES THE DOOR

"Come, my people, enter your chambers, and shut your doors behind you; hide yourselves for a little while until the fury has passed by."

- Isaiah 26:20

On May 22, 2011, an EF5 tornado carved a mile-wide path straight through Joplin, Missouri. With winds topping 200 miles per hour and crawling at a devastatingly slow pace of just 10 mph, it stayed on the ground for thirty-eight relentless minutes… shredding homes, toppling hospitals, and reducing entire neighborhoods to splinters. Yet in the midst of the devastation, a handful of small steel boxes dotted the landscape; unbroken islands in a sea of destruction.

When the sirens first began to wail, Tom Cook and his daughter, Ryanne, sprinted for the steel chamber bolted to their basement floor, a reinforced shelter built for a moment like this. They jumped inside, pulled the heavy door shut, and locked it behind them.

Outside, everything around them was coming apart; walls crumpled, glass exploded, beams snapped like twigs. For thirty-eight terrifying minutes, they could do nothing but wait as the monster clawed outside the door of their steel box, doing all it could to suck them out.

But the door held. Tom and his daughter were sealed in.

When the all-clear finally sounded, they opened the door to a world they could hardly recognize. Everything familiar was gone. But they were alive, still here because the door had done its job.

The Door That Divides

Centuries earlier, another family found themselves sealed safely behind a door. Their story, told in the opening chapters of Genesis, is so familiar that it's easy to miss the details. That's what happens with well-known stories, we stop listening closely. And in this one, there's a subtle line tucked between the monumental moments of animals marching two by two and water bursting up from the deep. But that line is both deliberate and significant:

> "Noah, the sons of Noah, and Noah's wife and the three wives of his sons, entered the ark...*and the Lord closed the door behind him*."[16]

The flood was coming. A new season was beginning. It was time for Noah and his family to go. No matter how much they may have wanted to stay with the only life

---

16. Genesis 7:13, 16

they had ever known, it was time to move on. And the door on that boat marked the divide between what was and what would be.

But notice who closed it. It wasn't Noah. That door didn't close by itself. It was God.

The author of the story wants us to see something: God is not just watching history unfold, He's the One orchestrating it. All doors belong to Him. This is the foundational truth on which everything else in this book rests: we serve a sovereign God who rules and reigns over times, seasons…and doors.

Seasons don't just change. Doors don't close accidentally. Daniel 2:21 says, "God alone changes times and seasons." Revelation 3:7 tells us that He shuts doors no man can open and opens doors no man can shut. God has determined our appointed times.[17]

This means behind every shifting season and every closed door, there is Someone in control. The door to Noah's ark didn't close arbitrarily. There was an appointed moment. And when that day came, God closed the door on Noah's season. There would be no going back.

This is great news for anyone staring at a closed door.

The Kindness of the Closed Door

We usually think of closed doors in a negative sense, especially when we want what's on the other side of that

17. Acts 17:26

closed door. But closed doors aren't denials. They are deliverance in disguise. It was the kindness of the Lord to close the door behind Noah. He was sealing his family off from everything that was about to take place outside of that boat.

There's a beautiful mercy in this.

Noah had zero control over what happened next, which meant there was absolute surrender to the God who determined what came next. That single, solitary door of the ark closed Noah and his family into the safest place on the planet.

This is what doors do: they protect us.

I don't need to convince you of the importance of your front door. When you and your family go to sleep tonight, no one argues about whether it should be closed. It's instinct. Basic protection. And in the same way, God won't move you into a new season until the door to your old season is firmly sealed. This is the kindness of the Lord.

We may not see it that way in the moment, but transitioning you to the next season cannot take place until the door to the previous season is properly sealed.

I imagine there were things Noah wanted to take with him into his next season that the sealed door protected him from. The man didn't live in a vacuum. There must have been relationships he and his family had with those around him. Friends he broke bread with. Kids he had seen grow up. Was Noah tempted to open the door? "I really enjoyed being with them, Lord. Why can't they come with me?"

As the waters rose outside of his closed door, I can only imagine that those outside the door would have done anything to get in: *Noah, open the door! Noah, it's me!* But the door didn't belong to Noah. Doors belong to God.

And here's the point: closed doors are the Lord's divine protection for us. There are things that, if we had our way, would come with us through the door. But not everything from one season is intended to move with you into the new season.

Take relationships, for example. Abraham invited someone into his next season that God never intended to be there. It slowed him down, and nearly derailed the promise.[18] I'm sure Abraham had good reasons for wanting to fit Lot through the door of his new season. But whatever the reason, Lot coming with Abraham caused all kinds of trouble. And it was only when Abraham shed the baggage of young Lot that he was able to move into his next season.

Sometimes, what can't come with us isn't a person, it's a part of us. Things that we have grown accustomed to or that have become part of us won't fit through the door of the next season. God's closed door protects us from bringing those things with us.

---

18. see Genesis 12:1

I picture a succession of doors the Lord has for us over the course of our lives. But the further along on the journey we go, the smaller the doors become.[19]

Things that may have always been part of us now become oversized for where God wants to take us. So in His kindness, He closes those things off behind the door of that season.

It's easy to think the lifestyle we have become used to will always be the way we live. But what happens when that lifestyle becomes too big for the calling of a new season? It could be the cushy job won't fit through the door, so it comes to an end. Or maybe the vacation home, the Saturday morning fishing trip, or the lack of self-discipline. Maybe your pride is too big to fit through the next door. Maybe you picked up offense or bitterness in your previous season. Perhaps an unanswered prayer caused your unbelief to grow.

Whatever it is, God wants to close those things off and protect you from carrying them any further.

When the Past Still Tastes Sweet

We don't always know what can't come with us. That's why God closed the door of the ark, not Noah. There are desires from past seasons that can ruin us if they remain unchecked. The memory of what once satisfied us still shapes our appetite.

---

19. If you read *Obedience, Suffering, & Reward,* then you're familiar with this concept. It was described as the "triangle of obedience".

There's a story in Numbers 11 that illustrates this vividly.

Israel was in the wilderness, caught between Egypt and Promised Land—free, but not yet planted. They were weary of eating the same thing day after day. Manna was fun at first, but now they wanted something new on the menu. Routine had dulled their wonder.

Traveling among them were some Egyptians who had joined the exodus after witnessing what YHWH had done with their Pharaoh. Scripture calls them a *mixed multitude*.

> "The mixed multitude who were among them yielded to intense craving; so the children of Israel also wept again and said: 'Who will give us meat to eat? We remember the fish which we ate freely in Egypt, the cucumbers, the melons, the leeks, the onion, and the garlic; but now our whole being is dried up; there is nothing at all except this manna!'"[20]

They still had the flavors of Egypt on their lips. They remembered the diet of their former days and began to crave what used to fill them. Their focus shifted from where God was taking them—a land flowing with milk and honey—to what they had left behind. And in doing so, they despised the current provision of the Lord. They treated the holy bread of angels as something common.[21]

20. Numbers 11:4-6
21. See Psalm 78:25

Incredibly, God gave them what they wanted. A great wind blew quail into the camp until they were surrounded by meat. But as they gave in to their craving and feasted on the flavors of yesterday, the Lord struck them with a plague. The desert graves that marked the space between where they were and where God was leading them were named *Kibroth Hattaavah*—"the graves of craving."

We all know that feeling of longing for what once was. But when God closes the door on a former season and begins leading us through transition, we must resist the urge to glorify what He has already buried.

The truth is, we rarely remember the past accurately. The discomfort of the present makes the old days look better than they were. Israel longed for Egypt, forgetting that Egypt was the place of their bondage.

And we're not all that different.

The door that keeps us from running back to what we can no longer see clearly is mercy. God closes those doors to protect us: sometimes from others, sometimes from ourselves, often from anything that competes for our affection.

Whatever is in competition with God for your heart will not be allowed to walk with you into what's next. That was true for Noah. It was true for Israel. And it's true for us. If there is something that has a hold on you and is competing for your worship, walking into your next season will depend on you letting go of it.

If money and possessions have a grip on you, Jesus is going to nail your bank account to the cross...for your good and for His glory.

If what others think of you is competing with what you think of Him, Jesus is going to nail your reputation to the cross.

If your 20-year plan is competing with what He has planned for you, Jesus is going to nail your yellow brick road to the cross.

This is His kindness. Everything He does is love. He closes the door on things that are holding you back from where He intends to take you.

And sometimes, that same kindness draws a line of separation.

Every closed door carries both mercy and division. It separates us from what must remain behind and, at the same time, invites those willing to trust Him to step forward. That's what the door of the ark was, a threshold of trust.

Doors Separate

Until the very last moment, the door of the ark remained open. There was no guard at the door. This wasn't like the Garden of Eden, sealed by cherubim and flaming swords. This was an open door on a massive wooden vessel standing in the middle of the desert. Anyone brave enough to believe Noah's story could walk on that boat.

Peter wrote in 2 Peter 2:5 that Noah was a "preacher of righteousness." Interestingly, we don't know any sermons Noah ever preached. In fact, we don't have *any* record of anything Noah ever said, except for the blessings he proclaimed over his sons before he died. Yet, Scripture says Noah was a *proclaimer* of righteousness.

How can this be?

For 120 years, every swing of Noah's axe declared a message of righteousness and the reality that in Him alone there is salvation. Every tree that Noah cut, and every nail that he hammered, testified that the God of Noah is kind and He is making a way of salvation, literally. And for anyone who would turn to Him, they would receive life from Him. *Come in through that open door, enter the salvation of this ark.*

There was coming a day when that door would close, and then it would be too late. That door would become a separation; those who were inside the door were *separated* unto life, those who were outside the door were *separated* unto death. Whether a person received life or death was entirely up to where they were standing when the door was closed.

Doors separate. Not out of harshness. But because there comes a time when delay becomes our decision.

Jesus tells a parable in Matthew 25 about ten virgins waiting for the Bridegroom to arrive. His arrival is delayed, something we'll talk more about in Chapter 5. You could say that the ten virgins are standing in their own liminal space; the bridegroom has promised to come, but he's just not there yet. When he finally arrives, it's around midnight. Five of the virgins still have enough oil in their lamps. And as the wedding begins, these five can go out to meet the bridegroom and enter the door of the celebration.

But the other five virgins? They've run out of oil. They didn't know how to handle their season of delay. So these five go to the market to buy more oil from the merchants. When they finally arrive at the wedding celebration, the door is closed. They knock; "Lord, it's us…let us in. Lord, we know you, we were faithfully waiting for you while you were delayed. We see our five friends inside; we waited with them, too. Please, let us in!"

"No. The door is closed. Everyone I know is inside this door. The fact that you're on the outside is a witness that I don't know you."

The door didn't just close, it revealed something that otherwise wasn't clear. Those who were outside weren't just late; they were unknown to the bridegroom. The door separated those who were his from those who weren't.

God's mercy often looks like a closed door.

Are we okay with God in charge of our doors? What do we make of a God who closes the door on things that we would bring with us if we were in charge? Can we bear the disappointment of not being able to bring our favorite things with us? Or do we respond like children when it's time to give up the pacifier?

God is looking for a people who will not be pacified by things He says may have served a purpose but are no longer appropriate. A people who will grow up into the ways of the kingdom. A mature people who know how to hold things lightly. A Hebrews 11-type people looking ahead for a city with foundations, whose builder and maker is God.[22] A people who recognize their citizenship is in an age *to come*.

We don't always get to choose when a door closes, but we do get to choose how we respond. We can trust the One who shuts doors no man can open, and believe the closed door is not the end, but the beginning of a sacred in-between. The ark wasn't just a place of safety from the flood; it was a place of renewal for the next season. And so is the liminal space God uses to hem us in. It may feel like thirty-eight minutes in the dark, with no way to measure how close the danger is. But when the latch finally lifts, you'll find the world changed, and you'll realize the closed door was the reason you're still standing.

The shelter behind God's closed door is holy ground, where God meets with those He's sealed in for a purpose. It's the liminal space between where you were and where God is taking you. And it's in this hallway, more than anywhere else, that God does His deepest work.

---

22. Hebrews 11:10

SECTION II

THE HALLWAY

THE THRESHOLD

Every journey with God eventually brings you here, to the fragile space between what was and what will be.

It's the pause between promises spoken and promises fulfilled, the hush after one season ends and before the next begins. It's where the echo of yesterday still lingers, but tomorrow hasn't yet found its voice.

The liminal space is God's workshop, His forge. It's where He dismantles the scaffolding of self-sufficiency and removes the baggage we didn't know we were carrying: the pride, the fear, the need to stay in control. It's where He quiets the noise that once made us feel productive, and rewrites who we are when everything familiar has been stripped away.

It may seem like nothing is happening here. But I assure you, everything is happening here.

This section is for those standing in the in-between, for the ones waiting for direction, aching for progress, praying for clarity, and wondering if they somehow missed it.

You haven't.

The hallway is where heaven takes its time.

CHAPTER 3

THE SACRED WORK OF WAITING

"There is nothing more noble or more blessed in the exercise of our free will than to use it in waiting upon God"

- Andrew Murray

There is an ancient Japanese story about a caterpillar who tried to fly. From the time he was young, he had heard stories whispered about other caterpillars growing wings. "Just stay the course," the young caterpillar told himself, "and you, too, will soar above the trees."

So when the time came to enter his cocoon, he didn't resist. He wrapped himself in stillness and waited. He was ready to become what he was born to be.

But the stillness lasted longer than expected. Days passed. Then weeks. And nothing.

No wings. No soaring. No evidence that anything was happening at all.

And so he started to wonder, *Did I do something wrong? Did I miss it?* He thought waiting would feel more like progress. But all he had was darkness and silence. And so the little caterpillar grew restless.

Eventually, impatience got the best of him. He twisted and pushed and forced his way out, convinced that surely, the time had come.

But when he emerged, he collapsed.

His wings hadn't finished forming. What was meant to be his launch became his limit. And though he had escaped the waiting, he had also forfeited everything it was supposed to produce.

He would never fly.

What the little caterpillar didn't realize was that waiting wasn't wasted time. It was the very thing shaping him into who he was designed to be.

The Waiting

How many times have we tried to break free from our own waiting season too soon? How often have we mistaken the cocoon for the problem? But just because you can't *see* the transformation doesn't mean it's not happening.

In the kingdom of God, waiting is one of God's favorite tools to mold us and shape us into the image of His Son.

And the moment we believe the lie that we should already be flying in the next season, we sabotage the very process that was meant to give us wings.

Okay, yes—super cheesy. But the metaphor soars.

I'll stop now.

You get the point. The ancient Japanese proverb (which may or may not be ancient *or* Japanese) captures something we all know, but still wrestle with. We tend to think progress should come faster than it does. I mean, come on, what fifteen-year-old doesn't think they're ready for a driver's license? But inflated self-confidence, left unchecked, turns eager teenagers into undisciplined adults who *still* believe they're more ready for the next season than they actually are.

And by "they," I mean me.

When I was fifteen, I took my parents' car out for a joyride. I was sure I was ready. I knew the roads. I had watched enough *Fast & Furious* to consider myself more than qualified. When Dad found out, he was seconds away from calling the police just so I'd learn a grown-up lesson. Thankfully, Mom talked him off the ledge.

I was convinced I was ready. I wasn't.

Here's the point: there's something in us that just wants to *arrive*. We treat waiting like filler, as if the destination is what matters, and the in-between is just dead space.

So we rush. We push. We try to make something happen.

But in reality, waiting *is* the happening. As John Ortberg said,

> "Waiting is not just something we have to do until we get what we want. Waiting is part of the process of becoming what God wants us to be."[23]

When all is said and done, we will spend more time *between* seasons than actually in a destination. Sociologists, psychologists, and organizational thinkers alike have noted a striking pattern: life is not a series of long, stable seasons interrupted by brief change. It's the other way around. At the end of our days we'll look back and see a string of transitions punctuated by brief moments of stability.

Warning: potentially dry but necessary scientific data ahead...

Studies in developmental psychology show that adults experience major transitions every 7 to 10 years.[24] The average person now changes jobs a dozen times in their lifetime.[25] And according to U.S. Census data, the average American will move nearly twelve times over the course of their lifetime.

---

23. John Ortberg, *If You Want to Walk on Water, You've Got to Get Out of the Boat* (Grand Rapids, MI: Zondervan, 2001), 157.
24. See Erik Erikson's studies on the psychosocial stages of development
25. See Bureau of Labor Statistics

That means over a dozen times of packing up, saying goodbye, and starting over—often in unfamiliar territory. And these aren't just sterile, logistical moves where the main concerns are practical (*"last time we didn't label the boxes good enough, we won't make that mistake again"*).

Each move is an emotional marathon...a slow, stretching endurance of the heart. You pace yourself through unseen miles of letting go. Every goodbye takes something out of you. Every new beginning asks for something different from you. Behind every address change is a decision about how you're going to move forward.

The data confirms what many of us feel but rarely acknowledge: transition is not an interruption of normal life, it's a defining feature of it. Identity, maturity, and even faith aren't formed solely in the stable seasons. They're formed in the unstable space between them.

And that space will be marked by extended times of waiting on God to open up the next season. So it's imperative that we learn to wait well. It's essential that we put our expectations in check. It's vital that we show the world what it looks like to trust in the God of times and seasons. As Dr. Robert Gladstone writes in his phenomenal book *A Time To Build*,

> "God's seeds take time to grow. That is one of the great scandals of Jesus' kingdom. When He does something wonderful He plants - seed goes

> into earth, buried. Patience is required during germination."[26]

The Inheritance That Couldn't Wait

The caterpillar thought he was ready. I've thought I was ready. And Jesus tells the story of another son who thought he was ready.

He was the younger of two brothers...the son who didn't want to wait. He was tired of living under his father's roof, tired of the rules, tired of the process. So he asked for his inheritance...early.

> "Father, give me the share of the estate that is coming to me."[27]

He wanted the reward without the refinement, the promise without the process.

Desiring the inheritance wasn't wrong. It was coming to him eventually. But the timing? That's where everything unraveled.

And so the father, *surprisingly*, gave it to him. Just handed it over. No lecture. No warning. No reminder that inheritance without maturity rarely ends well. I mean, really, not even a mention of Proverbs 20:21?[28]

---

26. Dr. Robert Gladstone, *A Time to Build* (Orlando, FL: Christ for All Nations, 2019), 19.
27. Luke 15:12
28. "An inheritance gained hastily at the beginning will not be blessed at the end."

The son packed his bags, left the waiting, and headed straight into a "far country." That's the Bible's way of saying the boy headed straight for Vegas.

And for a while, everything was great. Friends. Fun. Options. Life looked like freedom.

Until it didn't.

Until the money ran out.

Until the friends disappeared.

Until he found himself knee-deep in pig slop.

That's where shortcuts lead: into fields we were never meant to be in, feeding on things we were never meant to touch, wondering how we ended up so far from home.

All because he couldn't wait.

Eventually, the son came to his senses. He began the long walk home, rehearsing his confession, convinced he'd return home as a servant.

> "Father, I have sinned against heaven, and in your sight; I am no longer worthy to be called your son; treat me as one of your hired servants."[29]

I can imagine the boy repeating the confession over and over on his way home, to make sure he gets it right when he stands before his father. Surely, the father will be livid. Certainly, there is going to be some necessary

---

29. Luke 15:18-19

convincing. The father was a man of means, and having another servant in his house would be a good consolation to the humiliation the son must have caused him.

The son had his script prepared.

> "Father, I have sinned…I am no longer worthy… treat me…as one of your hired servants."

But the father wasn't having any of that "servant" stuff. Before the son has a chance to finish his confession, the father cuts him off,

> "This *son of mine* was dead and is now alive, lost and now found."

The son is greeted like the son he is.

That's grace. That's God. Even when we walk out early, He knows how to lead us and welcome us home.

But let's be clear: Jesus is not teaching us to squander our inheritance because the Father is full of endless mercy. By demanding something he wasn't ready for, the son caused real pain. His father grieved while his son was off squandering. His brother grew bitter. I'm sure there were things the son did while he was away that left marks on him. He experienced, and caused, unnecessary wounds. All because he refused to wait for something that was coming to him…in its appointed time.

The Tension of the Wait

Those who wait on God in the space between seasons are demonstrating great faith. They're refusing to lean on their own understanding. They're rejecting the impulse to make something happen. Their impatience, and the counsel of those around them, may be saying one thing, but God has said nothing of the sort. God remains silent.

God has no deadlines. He's in no hurry. And understanding this helps us confidently rest when His timeline is moving at a different pace than ours.

It takes faith to stand still when the God who is never in a hurry remains silent. It takes faith to wait on a God who may not see fit to tell you why, how long, or even *what* you're waiting for.

All you know is that where you used to be is no longer where He has you. And until the God who makes paths straight shows you the next step to take, you wait. That's what faith looks like in the hallway of waiting.

Priestly Waiting

Leviticus tells the story of the waiting that was to take place before a priest could step into his season of serving the Lord. It details a moment of in-between: the soon-to-be priest has been called out of civilian life, but they're not *yet* equipped to stand before the Lord. Sacrifices had to be made. Blood had to be applied. Ceremonies had to be performed.

And after all of that, there was one last thing before the priest was consecrated:

> "At the doorway of the tent of meeting, moreover, you shall remain day and night for seven days and keep the charge of the LORD."[30]

Seven days of waiting.

Seven days of doing nothing...nothing but standing still.

Art Katz says this about the priestly waiting of Leviticus 8,

> "In priestly waiting, every fleshly thing, every desire to perform and win some glory for ourselves, every lazy, fearful tendency to take the easy and cheap way out, will rise to the surface. A mind battle takes place, and thoughts come to mind of the practical things that need to be done and how the time should really be more usefully employed. To patiently dismiss those thoughts, and bring our minds to a place of rest in God... does not come readily."[31]

Gladstone puts it this way in *A Time to Build*,

> "Don't spiritualize your impatience and immaturity as 'hunger' or 'zeal.' Let God have His way. It is time to value maturity over

30. Leviticus 8:35-36
31. Art Katz, *Apostolic Foundations* (Bemidji, MN: Burning Bush Press, 2009), 36.

> circumstantial breakthrough so we can gain the wisdom found in that narrow, uncomfortable crevice between expectation and delay. Make it your ambition simply to know Jesus better within the circumstances you currently occupy. God will take care of the rest. When we rush ahead, we miss His will and slow down the process. But when we wait within God's timetable, we fulfill His will and expedite the process. O Yes, that's how God uses time. Patience hastens destiny while impatience postpones it."[32]

That last line…gold. Patiently waiting in the in-between can actually hasten destiny.

> "Imitate those who through faith and patience inherit the promises."[33]

> "One who hurries his footsteps errs."[34]

Patience secures the promise. Impatience only postpones what God intends to give.

The Sacredness of Waiting

Waiting isn't just a process of occupying time. It's a sacred space.

There is a radiance that forms in those who have waited on God when no one else sees the point. A kind of

---

32. Gladstone, *A Time to Build*, 37.
33. Hebrews 6:12
34. Proverbs 19:2

beauty that settles on the lives of those who are willing to be hidden, obscure, and still.

The difference between the holy and the mundane will be demonstrated by those who are marked by something that has engraved them deep in their guts.

Before we move on, we must examine the tattooing of the soul that happens when we give ourselves to the process of waiting on God. This is not a theoretical concept. What happens in the waiting is intimately personal. It shakes the parts of us that still think God works on our timeline.

The Plow of Waiting

When Israel was pinned between the Red Sea and Pharaoh's army, fear seized them.

Fear: the great enemy of anyone who has ever waited on God. The unrelenting gravitational pull of fear is either;

A) back to where you came from, or

B) headlong into the first thing that presents itself as a way out of the liminal space.

On the banks of the Red Sea, Israel cried out,

> "Were there no graves in Egypt? Leave us alone that we may turn back and serve the Egyptians!"[35]

35. Exodus 14:11–12

Translation: They chose *option A.* "Waiting on God is going to kill us, so let's run the white flag up the pole and turn back. It's better to find a way through the door God closed behind us than wait here and do nothing."

Moses responds to the foolishness of the moment with a command that will encourage anyone waiting in the space between:

> "Do not be afraid. Stand still, and see the salvation of the Lord... The Lord will fight for you; you need only to be silent."[36]

Do *not* fear. Stand still. Keep your eyes on the God who brought you here. He will do what only He can do. You only need to be silent.

That means Israel had to stop rehearsing their fears and entertaining alternatives. The moment called for silence, not strategy. Life and death are in the power of the tongue, and sometimes faith sounds like silence.

The Hebrew word that we translate as "be silent" is *haras*. It's a fascinating word that means more than just silent stillness.[37] It carries the weight of something much deeper, literally.

Haras means to engrave, to plow, to prepare.

In agricultural communities, plowing is always the first work of a new season, which is critical for harvest.

---

36. Exodus 14:13–14
37. See Judges 18:19 and Proverbs 17:28 for instances where haras is translated "be silent"

Plowing takes place in stages: first, it breaks up the fallow ground so the early rains can soften the earth. Then, once softened, the land is plowed again—deeper this time—to prepare it for seed.

That's what God was doing in His people on the shores of the Red Sea. He wasn't ignoring them. He was plowing them. New truths about YHWH had to be "engraved" on them. Their hearts were being scratched with the blade of the plower's questions: Who is this God who brought us here? Did He bring us out only to destroy us? Can He be trusted?

That's what waiting does. It tills the hard soil of unbelief. It engraves God's faithfulness into places where fear once lived. It prepares us for a harvest we can't yet see. With the impossibility of a good outcome staring us in the face, the silent *haras* of the divine plow tills and softens unbelief. The pressure marks us and engraves something on us that lasts forever; "I remember when God did what only God could do."

When you're hemmed in, when it feels like there's no way forward and no way back, don't be afraid. Stand still. You only need to be silent.

The plow is in the ground.

Our Season of Waiting

For me, one of the hardest parts about waiting is that it can so easily look like failure. I'm no longer doing *that*, but I'm not *yet* doing *this*. I'm in between.

"Well, what happened with *that*? You were so excited about *that*. There was so much promise with *that*. You messed up, didn't you? Ah, that's why you're doing *this* and not *that*, right?"

I had to wrestle with these feelings of failure when the Lord moved our family from the mission field of Iraq to a new mission field in California. In some ways, I'm still wrestling with them. There are things we have been believing for that have not yet come to pass. I've found myself at times complaining like Israel on the banks of the Red Sea; *were there no graves in Iraq, Lord*!

Ok, it's never been *that* bad. But in the moment, it sure felt like it.

When God began calling us to California, we were filled with hope and expectation. We had a sense of what He would do in the new season, and we wanted to share it with everyone. Truth be told, part of me also wanted to make sure those around us knew we were moving *forward*, not backward.

I remember sitting down with my wife, Lindsey, and recording a video to detail the bullet points of what we sensed was on the horizon. It's hard to watch that video now, not because we missed God, but because very few of those bullet points have come to pass. We're still waiting.

This chapter is just as much for me as it is for you.

Be that as it may, one of the things we *did* get right was leaning on the promise of Scripture. Psalm 37 became a lifeline for our family,

> "Rest in the Lord and wait patiently for Him... those who wait upon the Lord will *inherit* the land."[38]

The Bible doesn't teach us that the best strategists inherit the land. Or the most gifted communicators. Or the boldest visionaries.

Those who *wait* inherit.

And that word "inherit"...wow. The glaring implication of that word is that there must *first* be a death.

That's what waiting feels like. It's the death of ambition—the death of what we thought should have happened by now. Expectation dies on the vine of waiting.

The fact that Israel would rather turn back and choose slavery to Pharaoh shows that waiting in the liminal space is exactly what they needed. There was still too much life in them to move forward into the place God had prepared for them. The promised inheritance of a land flowing with milk and honey could never be received unless there was first a death to everything they learned in Egypt.

The same goes for those of us on this side of the cross.

Paul writes in Galatians 2:20,

---

38. Psalm 37:7, 9

> "I have been *crucified* with Christ. It's no longer I who live, but Christ who lives in me."

He tells the Corinthians that Jesus died for all,

> "...and those who live should *no longer live for themselves*, but for Him who died for them and rose again."[39]

When the hallway stretches farther than we can see, we wait.

When enemies close in, we wait.

When days turn to months, and months turn to years—and still we haven't seen what God has promised—we wait.

Surrendering to the process of waiting in the in-between feels like death to the things we didn't realize were still alive in us. But this is the way of inheritance.

Waiting in the liminal space is not a theological abstraction for our family. It's something we have wrestled through with God. There's a reason two words from Psalm 37 are printed on our license plate: "Rest" and "Wait." It's not so I drive slower. It's a daily reminder that the only way our family will arrive at what the Lord has promised is by resting in Him and waiting on His timing.

Isaiah says those who wait on the Lord "will renew their strength."[40]

---

39. 2 Corinthians 5:15
40. Isaiah 40:31

Not re-use. Not re-cycle. Re-*new*.

That tells me the strength that got me here isn't enough to take me where I'm going. *New* strength is needed for a new season. Waiting gives God the space to supply it. That's grace.

God never intended His people to be sustained by yesterday's bread. So He invites us to wait. He's a good Father who isn't going to allow us to be in situations where we'd run and grow weary. The waiting is an expression of His goodness. It builds up a strength that keeps us from fainting (more on this in the next chapter).

Waiting isn't the delay we think it is. It's the re-supply.

> "Therefore, the Lord will wait, that He may be gracious to you...blessed are all those who wait for Him."[41]

We know that the poor in spirit are blessed. We know that the meek and the merciful are blessed. But do we know that those who wait are blessed?

> "Indeed, we count them blessed who endure."[42]

What Waiting Produced in Wilbur

Let's end this chapter with one more story—one about an exceptionally bright young man named Wilbur. In 1885, he was accepted to Yale University. The sky was the

---

41. Isaiah 30:18
42. James 5:11

limit for what Wilbur could accomplish at an institution like Yale.

Wilbur also loved to play hockey.

Weeks before he was to leave for school, he was playing hockey with some buddies when he got smashed in the face so hard his front teeth were knocked out. Suddenly, instead of going off to Yale, Wilbur found himself depressed in bed waiting for his face to heal. His acceptance to Yale was rescinded as he convalesced at home for *two years*. To make matters more complicated, Wilbur's mother was terminally ill and needed his help. Rather than spending his days learning and living the Ivy League life, he cared for himself, tended to his sick mother, and stared out the window…a lot.

Wilbur didn't know what he was waiting for.

He was stuck between where he was, where he wanted to be but no longer could go, and the great big question mark of what he was going to do once he got out of bed.

While he waited, Wilbur found joy in watching the birds out of his bedroom window. The benefit of being stuck there was he could let his mind wander onto things he otherwise would have been too busy to consider; silly things like why those birds could fly but he couldn't.

Fascinated with the flight of his backyard birds, Wilbur began to devour books from his father's library. He learned about engineering, mechanical concepts, and even the limited knowledge available at the time on aviation.

When he had finally healed enough to move around, Wilbur began conducting experiments with his brother. They set out to determine if what was commonly known about aerodynamics was true.

Turns out it wasn't.

Wilbur and his brother built a wind tunnel in their garage and discovered that everything written at that time about aerodynamics was completely wrong. The brothers began conducting more experiments to unravel the mystery of flight.

What began in seed form during Wilbur's unplanned season of waiting took flight, *literally*, eighteen years later on December 17, 1903, as Wilbur watched his brother, Orville, fly like a bird for 59 seconds in Kitty Hawk, North Carolina.

Would man have ever flown if Wilbur Wright didn't spend two years waiting in his sickbed…staring out the window at birds? Sure. But look what Wilbur's season of waiting produced *in him*.

As Henri Nouwen said in *Finding My Way Home*,

> "A waiting person is a patient person. The word *patience* means the willingness to stay where we are and live the situation out to the full in the belief that something hidden there will manifest

> itself to us… Waiting, then, is not passive. It involves nurturing the moment, as a mother nurtures the child that is growing in her womb."

The Gift in the Delay

So what will you do while you wait?

Trust. Worship. Refuse to let the stillness make you cynical. Hold fast to the voice you last heard and resist the urge to manufacture what only God can do. Refuse to be afraid. Look at what God is doing around you. Lean into the cross and allow Him to crucify whatever flesh is still left in you, gasping for air.

If you're in the cocoon, stay in the cocoon.

If you're in the desert, tend the sheep.

If you're convalescing, or caring for someone who is, let patience finish forming your ideas.

And when the day comes—and it will—when the doors open and the wind shifts, you'll realize: the waiting didn't hold you back. It shaped your wings.

Last line, I know, super cheesy…couldn't help myself.

CHAPTER 4

NEW WINESKINS: THE TENDER WORK OF RENEWAL

"The Father in His kindness wants to cause the most callous places in your heart to become the most tender."

– Damon Thompson

In the late 13th century, English knights returning from campaigns in Wales and Scotland were often given a curious order by their commanders. Before they could return to the front lines, they were required to visit the royal blacksmith. But not for new armor. They needed to tend to their swords.

After weeks in battle, the blades were worn down. The handles nicked. The swords, though still functional, had lost their edge. The sword had served well. But if it were ever to serve again, it couldn't stay as it was.

It may seem counterintuitive to pull a soldier during war, but wise commanders know the deadly consequences of assuming soldiers will tend to the fundamentals on their own.

Before the blacksmith could resharpen the blade, it first had to be reshaped. The weapon needed to become vulnerable again. So the steel was thrust into fire until it glowed red-hot, softening what combat had hardened. Then came the hammering; measured, deliberate blows reshaping what had been dulled by war. Finally, the blade was plunged into oil to seal it and temper the steel.

To the untrained eye, the process could be mistaken for destruction. To the impatient heart, it seemed like a waste of time. But to the blacksmith, it was simply the process of renewal.

The Renewal of Wineskins

Jesus says in Mark 2:22,

> "No one puts new wine into old wineskins; or else the new wine bursts the wineskins, the wine is spilled, and the wineskins are ruined. But new wine must be put into new wineskins."

Obviously, Jesus isn't giving us wine-making tips. He uses this illustration as a metaphor to teach us a profound spiritual reality.

Many of us have heard this parable. We understand that we are the wineskin, and what Jesus gives us, or "pours out," is the new wine. Jesus is teaching us that, just like the new wine in need of a new wineskin, when God begins to pour out something new—say, for example, the Messiah coming to set His people free from sin and death—the old wineskin of tradition and man-made religion will not be sufficient enough to receive the blessing of what God is doing. The old will break under the pressure of the new.

But here's the part we often miss about this passage: Jesus uses *two different words* for "new." By translating both of those words as "new," we miss the full weight of what He is saying.

The word Jesus uses for "new wine" is *neon*—something that is chronologically new. Recent. Fresh. That which has not been before. The shiny new car at the dealership is *neon*...until next year's model rolls in.

The word he uses for "new wineskin" is *kainos*—not new in time, but new in quality. Renewed. Restored. Made new *again*.

The wine is brand new.

The wineskin is *re*newed.

In ancient times, old wineskins weren't thrown away. They were too valuable for that. For hours, sometimes even days, the hides were soaked in oil, massaged, stretched, and reworked. It was often tedious and hidden work. There was nothing glamorous about it. But it was vital. Without the oil, the vessel would rupture under the pressure of new wine.

This is so crucial: Jesus isn't saying discard the old wineskin and replace it with something shiny and unused. He's saying that which has become calloused needs to be softened and made vulnerable again. The vessel needs to be *renewed.*

This is the work God does in the delicate liminal space. This is the blacksmith's forge of renewing what's been worn down in battle. It's the slow, hidden softening of a heart that's grown tough, the stretching of trust, the reworking of desires until they're aligned again with His. The hallway between seasons becomes the place where God gently, persistently, shapes us into vessels that can bear the weight of His new wine.

It's in that fragile middle where God says, "I love what you held. But if you want to hold what I'm about to pour next, you have to let Me soften you again."

Why Renewal Matters

When we come to faith in Christ, Scripture says that we are born again, *made new*,

> "If anyone is in Christ, he is a new (*kainos*) creation; old things have passed away, behold, all things have become new (*kainos*)."[43]

That's the identity of every believer. We are in Christ, and by way of that submersion into Him, we have been reborn in the image of God's original design.

---

43. 2 Corinthians 5:17

And as we move through the challenges of life, God intends that we would continually expose ourselves to the baptism of His oil to remain tender. If we don't, like the wineskin, we become hardened, brittle, and unfit to contain what God wants us to carry. It doesn't mean we aren't saved. But like a battle-worn sword, if we don't step away for renewal, we can become ineffective.

The space between where you were and where God is taking you is His designed moment for renewal.

Every season leaves its mark. Some wounds are obvious. Others hide behind layers of self-preservation and cynicism. But all of us, if we're honest, can become a little calloused with each passing season. The trials of life can bruise us. The people around us can disappoint us. Our own unmet expectations can quietly calcify our hearts.

Renewal isn't a luxury. It's a necessity. But nothing becomes tender by accident. It requires fire. Oil. Time. Stillness. It can't be faked. No amount of gifting, self-discipline, or ambition can replace the work God does in the quiet basin of renewal. Like the sword removed from battle, the process of renewal demands a pause.

You can't be reshaped while you're still swinging.

And herein lies the reason so few can hold new wine: we refuse to pause long enough for God to do the necessary work of tending to our wounds, correcting our errors, resetting our rhythms. So we keep swinging with dull blades, thinking it's just too costly to stop.

I once heard a story of a young lumberjack determined to prove himself. On his first day, he cut down more trees than anyone else. Encouraged by his success, he continued to work harder and longer each day. But as the days went on, his productivity began to decline.

So he tried harder. He worked even longer hours. Still, the number of trees he cut down continued to decline.

An older, more experienced lumberjack noticed and pulled him aside.

"I don't understand," the ambitious young man said. "I'm working harder than ever. Why am I falling behind?"

The old man smiled. "When was the last time you sharpened your axe?"

Some things only find their strength again when you stop long enough to tend to them.

The liminal space is God's way of slowing us down enough to renew our hearts so we can move into the next season the way God intends for us to.

> "Create in me a clean heart, O God, and renew a right spirit within me."[44]

My Own Tenderizing

I remember well one of the more difficult transition seasons the Lord brought me through. I knew God was softening the places in my heart that were on the verge

44. Psalm 51:10

of cracking. It was one of those rare times when I had the conscious awareness in real-time that God was doing a deep work in me.

The previous season was fraught with struggle and disappointment. I carried deep wounds of betrayal. My heart had already begun to harden when, mercifully, God slammed the door on that season and began to hold me in a way I had never experienced.

I found myself in the hands of the heavenly Blacksmith.

As I took inventory of what happened in the previous year, God drew so near to me. My heart felt incredibly tender. I remember sitting in a coffee shop in Santa Maria, California having a conversation with someone I had literally just met. As I shared with him the story of how I came to know Jesus, I began to cry when I told him how my wife had prayed me into the kingdom. I never cry. Never. And definitely not in coffee shops with someone I just met. But it was a cathartic moment of healing as I recalled the Lord's faithfulness in my life over the years. The previous season's difficulties were put in their proper perspective.

During those months of being held between seasons, I knew I was being held by the Comforter in a unique way. To leave that space of renewing and tenderizing for the sake of getting on with whatever was coming next was the farthest thing from my mind. I wanted to remain in the hands of the Lord as He renewed my soul and restored my heart. It felt like being on an extended fast. You know it will end, but once you experience the tenderness that comes from tucking away with Jesus, you stop longing for release.

A fascinating thing happened to me during that season of renewal: the Lord began waking me up at 5:37 in the morning. For multiple days in a row, my eyes would pop open at the same time, 5:37. I've learned that this is one of the ways the Lord draws my attention to a particular passage of Scripture.

After a couple days of these 5:37 wake-up calls, I had a sense that there was something for me in the gospels. I checked Matthew 5:37,

> "But make sure your statement is, 'Yes, yes' or 'No, no'; anything beyond these is of evil origin."

Great verse, but it didn't speak to my season of renewal I was experiencing. How about Mark 5:37?

> "And He allowed no one to accompany Him except Peter, James, and John, the brother of James."

No, that couldn't be it. How about Luke 5:37?

> "And no one pours new wine into old wineskins; otherwise the new wine will burst the skins and it will be spilled out, and the skins will be ruined."

Bingo. That was a word in season. There was something new that God was going to pour out, but the wineskin of my heart needed to be prepared first. It was the goodness of the Blacksmith to shut me in His workshop and expose me to the fires of refinement and the oil of His presence. I knew I was safe in His hands.

I leaned in and allowed the chisel of His word to reshape me. He softened the hardened edges that had formed because of the previous season. There was nowhere else I wanted to be but in the hands of the faithful Blacksmith.

Renewal doesn't just make the vessel soft again; it makes it ready to receive again.

What God restores, He always intends to use. And sometimes the most merciful thing He can do is hold us still long enough to make us tender again.

That season of being hemmed in taught me something deeper about renewal. It wasn't just that God was softening what had grown brittle in me…it was that He was inviting me to be emptied. To release what I had carried. To let go of the last season, even the parts that still felt useful.

Because renewal doesn't come just by being made soft again; it comes when the vessel is willing to be *poured out*…something we'll discuss next.

CHAPTER 5

THE EMPTYING

"I will go through an emptying phase, as difficult and challenging, and as much humility as that may require, to say everything I'm in possession of is not all there is."

- Damon Thompson

In 1975, inside a lab in Rochester, New York, a twenty-four-year-old engineer named Steve Sasson built something extraordinary. It was awkward, cobbled together with scavenged parts, and about the size of a toaster, but it could do what no other camera in the world could do: take a picture without film.

Sasson had built the first digital camera.

The young engineer showed the invention to the top brass of his company, certain he was showing them the future of photography. He demonstrated how the lens captured light, how the image was converted into digital signals, and how it could be displayed on a screen. It was rudimentary. Grainy. Black and white. But it worked.

And that was the problem.

The executives weren't impressed. They were scared.

The dilemma was Sasson didn't work for just some random company. He worked for Kodak. And almost 90% of Kodak's revenue came from the traditional analog process this little box threatened to make obsolete: film, darkroom chemicals, and photographic paper.

So they buried it.

Kodak downplayed the potential of what would become one of the most marketable inventions of our time. They couldn't stomach the thought of being emptied of what had made them successful.

It took some time, but eventually someone else developed their own digital camera, and by the early 2000s, digital photography exploded. Competitors like Canon, Nikon, and Sony surged ahead. By 2003, digital cameras outsold film cameras for the first time. Then, in 2007, a little product called the iPhone put a digital camera in everyone's back pocket. The revolution had begun. By the time Kodak finally pivoted, it was too late. They filed for bankruptcy in 2012.

Kodak didn't fail for lack innovation. They failed because they couldn't be emptied. They thought it would cost too much to pivot. The emptying of all that they had known about manufacturing photography equipment would mean loss—of control, of reputation, of predictability. When something new was being poured out in the world around them, Kodak held on to the old, convinced that the old was still better.

That same pattern plays out in the human heart during the delicate seasons of transition. We cling to what's familiar, what once worked. We fear the loss of what we've known more than we trust the promise of what God wants to do next. Like Kodak, we risk missing new wine in new seasons because we're unwilling to be emptied of the old. But in the kingdom of God, what once served you can start to suffocate you if you're not willing to let go.

The Delicate Emptying

There's always a fundamental moment of transition between outpourings. It's the period when what used to be new wine stops flowing *for the benefit* of the wineskin. It's a season of grace for the wineskin to be renewed so that even *newer* wine can be received.

Now, here's the tension, and why so few discern that decisive moment. In Luke's account of the wineskin parable, Jesus says this,

> "No one, having drunk old wine, desires new; for he says, '*The old is better.*'"[45]

That's the rub. We love what we had. We cherish the old wine. And it's right to honor what God poured out in a previous season, whether that's a revival, an anointed individual or movement, or the way we've done things

45. Luke 5:39

and watched God's blessings flow. But the temptation is to cling to the old wine, to keep sipping from yesterday's grace and call it "better." To prefer what God *did*, while ignoring what He still wants to do. As the old saying goes, the greatest enemy of tomorrow's move of God is yesterday's move of God.

If we're going to move forward into the purposes of God, we simply can not be married to what He did in a previous season. We can not build monuments to the past.

The irony is this: only those who are willing to be emptied can carry something better than what they had before. Because new wine doesn't stay new forever.

Leonard Ravenhill, in discussing the process of God stripping His people of things they have picked up in previous seasons, said, "Most Christians pray to be blessed; few pray to be broken." To which I would add: few pray to be emptied, either.

Are we willing to give up all that we are in order to possess all that He is?

The Example of Israel

In the early days of Israel's story, when they were still just a family of seventy or so people, a famine nearly cut off their future. The land of promise, the place God had sworn to give them, couldn't sustain them yet. So they went down to Egypt.

What they found there was more than grain.

They found Joseph, the son they thought was lost.

They found favor with Pharaoh.

They found provision, shelter, and space to grow.

Egypt was their salvation.

> "So Israel dwelt in the land of Egypt, in the country of Goshen; and they had possessions there and grew and multiplied exceedingly."[46]

God had used Egypt to preserve His people. It was a place of rescue, a gift of grace for a desperate season.

But Israel stayed too long in the blessing, and eventually, what saved them became the very thing that enslaved them.

A new Pharaoh rose up who didn't remember Joseph. Chains replaced provision. Whips replaced favor. What began as salvation became a barrier to the blessing they were meant to become.[47]

That's what happens when we hold on to what God once used instead of holding on to God Himself. Egypt was never meant to be permanent; it was provision for a famine, not a foundation to build upon.

---

46. Genesis 47:27
47. See Genesis 12:3

But comfort is seductive. We start building homes where God meant for us to pitch tents. And slowly, what was once grace becomes bondage.

If God's people were going to move forward into their identity as the people through whom salvation's blessing would flow to the nations, they needed to be emptied of the blessing of the previous season.

And this wasn't a one-time instance, either.

When Israel was finally delivered out of Egypt, they received something precious from God: the Law. Engraved in stone by the hand of God Himself, the Law was a gift for the newly liberated people of God; a framework for life, identity, and worship. It was fresh. It was sacred. It was *new wine* for a new season.

But what began as a gift became a burden.

When the time came to receive something even better than the Law—life through Jesus—they clung to what they had, insisting it was better. They refused to be emptied of the old. The very thing that once marked them as God's people now stood in the way of His salvation.

> "By the deeds of the law no flesh will be justified, for by the law is the knowledge of sin."[48]

The Law wasn't wrong, it was just over. Its assignment had ended. It had preserved them until the fullness of time had

48. Romans 3:20

come. It revealed sin, but couldn't remove it. It was never intended to. The Law was a shadow. And when the very Substance of life stood in front of them, they couldn't let go of the old. They refused to be emptied.

And so the question lingers: How can something used by God for blessing in one season become bondage in another?

Before we answer that, let's look at another (*unbelievable!*) example from Scripture. A symbol of salvation that outlived its season. A relic that became an idol.

The Bronze Serpent

In Numbers 21, during the time of Israel's journey through the wilderness, they became discouraged. That discouragement quickly turned into grumbling against Moses…and God,

> "Why have you brought us up out of Egypt to die in the wilderness? There is no food (*there was*) and no water (*there was*), and our soul loathes this worthless bread (*they meant the bread of heaven that God supernaturally gave them every morning*)."[49]

The response to Israel's grumbling was fiery serpents. Many were bitten by the snakes and died.

49. Numbers 21:5

> "Therefore, the people came to Moses, and said, 'We have sinned, for we have spoken against the Lord and against you; pray to the Lord that He take away the serpents from us."[50]

So the Lord told Moses to make a bronze serpent, place it on a pole, and lift it high. Whoever was bitten and looked upon it would live.

Salvation came from looking at a prophetic symbol; a foreshadowing of the day when the Messiah Himself would be lifted up for the healing of all who look to Him.

Pretty remarkable.

But fast-forward nearly a thousand years. In 2 Kings, we read about King Hezekiah, a righteous reformer who tore down Israel's idols and false altars:

> "He removed the high places and broke the sacred pillars (*the places where God's people had worshipped false gods*), broke down the wooden images (*their idols*), and broke in pieces the bronze serpent that Moses had made; for until those days the children of Israel burned incense to it, and called it Asherah."[51]

Did you catch that? The very object God once used as a vessel of healing had become an idol of worship. What once pointed them to God had become a replacement for Him. Rather than leaving the serpent in the sands

---

50. Numbers 21:7
51. 2 Kings 18:4

of the wilderness, Israel carried it with them…and eventually bowed down to it.

This is the temptation of God's people, both ancient and modern. God moves powerfully, and if we're not careful, we place the instrument of His mercy on a pedestal. Idolatry is rarely obvious; sometimes it looks like loyalty to what used to work. We cling to the blessing long after it's time to move on, refusing to let it be buried in the soil of that season. By doing so, *we* become out of season.

David understood this. The same man that used a slingshot to defeat Goliath never reached for it again. He wasn't called to build a kingdom with what had killed the giant. He knew that what God used in one battle might not be what God would use in the next.

When David's enemies rose up against him, David didn't assume. He prayed.

> "And David inquired of God, saying, 'Shall I go up against the Philistines? Will You deliver them into my hand? The Lord said to him, 'Go up, for I will deliver them into your hand.'"[52]

And when the enemy returned, David didn't recycle his last revelation.

> "David inquired again of God, and God said to him, 'You shall *not* go up after them; circle around them, and come upon them in front of the

52. 1 Chronicles 14:10

> mulberry trees. And it shall be, when you hear a sound of marching in the tops of the mulberry trees, then you shall go out to battle, for God has gone out before you."[53]

What worked last time wasn't going to work this time. Yesterday's strategy had to be emptied so today's instructions could be received.

As Damon Thompson said, "God will ask you to empty yourself of good things you've encountered that are keeping you from the ultimate thing you were designed for."

God may have used Egypt to save you. He may have used the Law to shape you. He may have used the bronze serpent to heal you or the slingshot to deliver you. But if you keep clutching to what He used last time, you may miss what He wants to do this time. The wineskin must be emptied before it can be renewed.

That's why the last words of every move of God are always the same: *we've never done it this way before.*

Your next season doesn't begin with a filling. It begins with an emptying.

Otherwise, you risk starving to death...with a full stomach.

---

53. 1 Chronicles 14:14-16

The Whale That Starved While Full

In March of 2019, a forty-foot whale washed ashore on the island of Mindanao in the southern Philippines. Villagers gathered to see the massive creature, assuming it had died of natural causes.

But when marine biologists performed the necropsy, they uncovered something tragic.

Inside the whale's stomach was eighty-eight pounds of plastic: shopping bags, rice sacks, nylon rope, even a pair of flip-flops. The animal had starved to death… *with a full stomach*.

Its body was full, but not with anything that could nourish it. It was packed with all the wrong things, things it had mistaken for food. It had consumed what felt like nourishment, but in the end, those things robbed it of the ability to receive what it truly needed.

The scientists called it "the worst case of plastic ingestion" they had ever seen. But it's more than a marine tragedy.

It's a parable.

It's a haunting picture of what can happen in the liminal space. God wants to empty us of the things we've picked up along the way; habits, fears, opinions, offenses, even blessings from the last season that now sit heavy in the soul.

We may not be full of plastic, but we can be full of pride. Full of methods that once worked but no longer fit. Full of assumptions, coping mechanisms, and residue from what used to feed us.

We can become so stuffed with yesterday's manna that there's no room for today's bread.

Until we allow God to empty us, we'll keep mistaking fullness for health, and the very things we *think* are sustaining us will be the things that keep us from moving forward.

When I Was Emptied

When I was in Bible school, there were many things the Lord wanted to empty from my wineskin. In their proper season, most of them were good things that had served me well. Others were distortions, wrong ideas about who God is. I wanted Him so badly. I was hungry to know Him, to experience His presence, to be used by Him to touch those around me.

One night, I was up late praying. I lived an hour from campus, and the school's director and his wife were kind enough to let me stay in their tiny guest room after Tuesday classes. I remember being on the floor that night, hemmed in between the wall and the bed, barely enough space to kneel. Looking back, it was the perfect picture of my walk with God at that time: pressed between what I knew and what I longed for, surrounded by walls of old ideas and muscle memory that felt immovable.

My prayer that night was simple: "Lord, I just don't want to be deceived."

I believed there was more of God than I had allowed Him to be, but I was afraid of the unfamiliar. I was learning things about Him that were new, outside the boundaries of what I had grown up with. They were untested. What if I opened myself to something false?

Samuel Whitefield writes this in *Will You Choose the Wilderness*,

> "Our confidence in our own ability is an expression of pride, and it limits our ability to experience the power of God...There are some things so precious to Him that He will not bring them to pass until we have been emptied of our confidence in human strength and have nothing left but intercession."[54]

Through the intercession of those Tuesday nights on the floor of the Collins' tiny guest room, the Lord led me into precious things. He showed me that what I had was not all there is. He patiently dealt with my fears, spoke to my heart in unmistakable ways, and gave me the grace to be emptied.

In place of the old, He gave me the new: new relationships, a new calling, new depths of understanding about who He is and what His kingdom is like. From where I stand now, it's almost inconceivable to think I would have clung so tightly.

---

54. Samuel Whitefield, *Will You Choose the Wilderness* (Grand View, MO: OneKing Publishing, 2021), 30.

God led me through that transition like the good Shepherd He is. He was patient enough with His pace to keep me confident in His character, and He stretched me enough to keep me moving forward.

If you find yourself in that place, caught between what was and what will be, trust Him with the emptying.

How often have we cried out for something new while clutching the very things God is trying to remove? We say we want revival but keep our hands on routines and traditions. We ask for transformation but insist on keeping our preferences intact. And like those in Luke 5, we live as if the old is better.

It's like renovating a house. You can't renovate without making a mess. That's why so many people with the means to renovate stay in outdated homes; they don't want the disruption. There are memories hanging on the walls that would have to come down, a favorite armchair that won't match the new decor, a dent in the baseboard that reminds them of when the kids were little.

So instead of enduring the temporary inconvenience that brings renewal, they settle for nostalgia. They choose comfort over change.

It's the same in the kingdom. When God begins to bring something new, we cling to the familiar—the relationships, the memories, the safety blankets—believing the old is better. But God will not pour new wine into an old vessel. He loves us too much to do that. So He waits. He withholds the new wine until the wineskin has been made new enough to hold it.

As A.W. Tozer wrote,

> "We must of necessity be a people who are empty enough for God to fill, weak enough for God to strengthen, and surrendered enough for God to use."

Moses Between Egypt and the Mountain

Moses was a man who knew what it was like to be poured out.

He grew up in Pharaoh's house; educated, connected, and confident. There were many things that had served him well in Egypt, but those same things would not get God's people into the Promised Land. In fact, what Moses learned in Pharaoh's palace would have to be unlearned before he could lead God's people in freedom.

> "Now it came about in those days, when Moses had grown up, that he went out to his fellow Hebrews and looked at their hard labors; and he saw an Egyptian beating a Hebrew, one of his fellow Hebrews. So he looked this way and that, and when he saw that there was no one around, he struck and killed the Egyptian, and hid his body in the sand."[55]

55. Exodus 2:11-12

We'll talk about this more in the next chapter, but for now, let's just say when we first encounter Moses in the Bible he is acting more like an Egyptian prince than the most humble person on the face of the earth.[56] So how does Moses go from murderer to man of God?

Forty years on the back side of the desert, that's how.

Forgotten by Egypt. Unrecognized by Israel. Just tending sheep in the middle of nowhere.

The wilderness was Moses' hallway of emptying.

He had to be poured out before he could be filled with what God was going to do next. Familiarity with Pharaoh's house had to be forgotten before the blueprints of God's house could be received. Humility had to slay the murderer.

As Andrew Murray wrote, "Pride must die in you, or nothing of Heaven can live in you."[57]

The deliverance of Israel didn't begin when Moses was at his most confident; it began when he was at his most surrendered. That's the way of the wineskin.

If you find yourself in that place now, between what was and what's next, you're in good company. Moses found God there. And so will you.

---

56. Numbers 12:3
57. Andrew Murray, *Humility: The Beauty of Holiness*, Chapter 2 — "Humility: The Secret of Redemption" (1895).

As Charles Spurgeon once said,

> "Such mature men… could scarcely have been produced if they had not been emptied from vessel to vessel, and made to see their own emptiness and the vanity of all things around them."[58]

If you're still holding on to what got you here, hold it loosely. God despises mixture. That's a strong statement, but it's true. Whole-hearted devotion and surrender are what delights the Lord.[59] If you're clinging to what worked in a previous season, be prepared that God may ask you to let go before He can move you into what's next.

> "He's not going to top your old off with his new. Therefore, there's going to be a preliminary process called emptying, and for me, every time he comes with something new, he requires me to let go of something old…Paul said, 'I put those things that are in the past behind me.' If it's in the past, it's already behind you. But many of you still have your past in front of you, and we need to learn to put our past behind us, or we're never going to be able to press toward the mark of the

---

58. Charles Spurgeon, Commentary on Jeremiah 48:11, in The Treasury of the Old Testament: Jeremiah and Lamentations(London: Passmore & Alabaster, 1893).
59. See Deuteronomy 22:9-11, Psalm 119:2, 10; Jeremiah 29:13, 2 Corinthians 6:14

> prize of the high calling of God that is in Christ Jesus."[60]

So let us press on, throwing off everything that hinders.[61]

The Emptying of Jesus

Let's look at one last example from Scripture before we move on. In Philippians 2, Paul gives us a glimpse into one of the most profound mysteries in all of Scripture: the self-emptying of Christ.

Before the Incarnation, Jesus existed eternally in perfect unity with the Father; equal in majesty, glory, and power. Yet in a staggering act of humility, He emptied Himself of the rights and privileges that came with being the eternal Son of God. He didn't stop being God, He simply refused to leverage His divinity for personal gain.

Paul writes,

> "Have this attitude in yourselves which was also in Christ Jesus, who, as He already existed in the form of God, did not consider equality with God something to be grasped, but emptied Himself by taking the form of a bond-servant and being born in the likeness of men. And being found in appearance as a man, He humbled Himself by becoming obedient to the point of death: death on a cross."[62]

---

60. Damon Thompson, sermon preached at The Homestead Mobile, 2024
61. Hebrews 12:1
62. Philippians 2:5–8 (NASB)

The Greek word for "emptied" here is *kenoō*—to pour out, to make void, to divest.

Jesus willingly poured Himself out. He traded His throne for a manger, His glory for swaddling cloth. And even then, He didn't stop. He kept pouring…through Gethsemane, through the whipping post, through the cross.

God became a man. Because of love, He wrapped Himself in flesh so that He could bleed for us. The Son gave Himself entirely to the purpose of the Father, who had determined in eternity past that without the shedding of blood there is no forgiveness of sins.[63]

God can't bleed, and men can't save. So what is Love to do but empty Himself and come in the likeness of a bleeding Man.

Why does this matter in a chapter about our emptying?

Because God never asks anything of us that He hasn't already endured Himself.

The emptying Christ underwent is beyond comprehension. We will never grasp the full depths of what Jesus laid down. But Paul doesn't offer this passage simply to inspire us. He offers it as an invitation:

> "Let this mind be in you…"

---

63. Hebrews 9:22

He emptied Himself. So must we.

If the One who spoke galaxies into being chose to lay it all down for love, then surely we can let go of the things we're still clinging to. Whether it's comfort, reputation, familiarity, or control, none of it compares to the glory on the other side of surrender.

Jesus shows us that emptying is never loss when the One inviting you to be poured out is as kind as our Savior is.

> "Therefore God has highly exalted Him and given Him the name above all names."[64]

64. Philippians 2:9

CHAPTER 6

DELAY REVEALS DESIRE

"The Lord will never give the witness unless we believe; and if we believe, we can afford the delay."

— Rees Howells

There's a story told among farmers about the bamboo tree.

When a bamboo seed is planted, there are no immediate signs of life. The ground remains bare and unchanged for months. You water it. You tend the soil. You protect the seed from pests and drought. And still…nothing.

A year passes. Then another. Nothing but dirt.

Yet day after day, the bamboo farmer returns to that same patch of ground, watering what looks like failure.

Another year passes. Then year four. Still nothing.

By the fifth year, most would walk away. The logical conclusion, which no one would fault you for, is that the seed failed.

But those who understand the way of bamboo know what's happening *beneath* the surface.

In those first years, an enormous root system is spreading underground, anchoring itself to support what's on the way. It's unseen work. Deep work. Work that can't be measured.

Then, sometime in that fifth year, everything changes. The bamboo shoots up—often over *ninety feet* in just six weeks.

To the casual passerby, it looks like overnight success. But there was nothing sudden about it. What looked instantaneous was simply the unveiling of hidden formation.

The Discipline of Delay

In the Kingdom of God, transitions work the same way. There are precious seasons when God asks us to trust Him without any visible progress. Everything looks barren, and the temptation to move or manufacture growth becomes overwhelming.

Delay stirs up every unspoken expectation we carry about how long our transition *should* take. It exposes our assumptions about how quickly God should move when we've already said yes.

And if we're not careful, we'll do just what Israel did at Sinai when the delay lasted longer than expected.

The Mount Sinai Incident

Exodus 32 tells the story of Moses on Mount Sinai, a story that actually begins back in chapter 19. Forty days earlier, Moses had climbed the mountain to meet with God: to receive the Law and, unknowingly, to encounter His glory.[65]

Meanwhile, the people waited below.

So while Moses was wrapped in glory, Israel was covered up in uncertainty.

> "Now when the people saw that Moses *delayed* to come down from the mountain…"[66]

Moses delayed.

Interesting phrase. Delay implies there was a specific timeline in mind. If I show up late to lunch and apologize for being delayed, it means there was an agreed time I was expected to arrive.

Question: What's the standard duration one should expect to meet with God on mountaintops?

Not sure what the handbook says about that, but make no mistake, Israel had a timeline in mind.

And Moses was late.

---

65. See Exodus 24:18
66. Exodus 32:1

> "Now when the people saw that Moses delayed coming down from the mountain, the people assembled around Aaron and said to him, 'Come, make us a god who will go before us; for this Moses, the man who brought us up from the land of Egypt—we do not know what happened to him.'"[67]

The delay made Israel irrational; *We don't know what happened to Moses.*

Maybe he got lost.

Maybe he went to the Promised Land without us.

Maybe God killed him.

There are powerful, internal forces at work when we're delayed and don't know what's happening. Our minds begin racing, and we imagine every scenario that could be playing out behind the scenes while we sit around twiddling our thumbs. Imagination becomes an idol factory.

When things didn't fit Israel's timeline, fear began to write it's own story: *If we're alone in this wilderness, we need a god to lead us out of here.*

> "And Aaron said to them, 'Break off the golden earrings'... and he fashioned it with an engraving tool, making a molded calf. Then they said, 'This

67. Exodus 32:1

> is your god, O Israel, that brought you out of the land of Egypt!'"[68]

Israel didn't abandon God, they just remade Him. They reshaped Him into something more manageable. Something a bit more predictable.

Something that could get them out of the hallway between Egypt and the Promised Land.

The golden calf wasn't just a rebellion against God. It was a rebellion against *delay*. It was a refusal to live in the tension of uncertainty. It was impatience dressed up as worship. It looked like devotion, but it was desperation. Israel borrowed the language of reverence so they could keep singing and dancing, but because they refused God's delay, their worship was redirected to a god they could carry instead of one they had to follow.

And none of us is immune to that temptation.

We read this story and think it's absurd to imagine we would do such a thing. But just because we've never melted down jewelry and fashioned false idols doesn't mean we haven't tried to remake God into an image more agreeable to our expectations of who He should be.

A god who moves according to *our* pace.

A god who validates *our* urgency.

A god who blesses *our* impatience.

---

68. Exodus 32:2-4

Any attempt to escape the liminal space in our own strength is us following a god of our own making. When we force our way out of the hallway, we are not following the God who led us there.

Delay Reveals Desire

The story of Israel and the golden calf exposes a sobering truth about God's people: they didn't want God, not God as He actually is.

And that's the power of delay: it reveals what we truly desire.

The liminal space serves to strip away things that usually pad my desire with distraction. If I want the security of having something I can run to when things are hard, like a god who fixes my problems in the allotted time I set for him, then delay will expose my desire for a god made in my image. When my version of "god" stops performing on schedule, I'll simply abandon him for one who will.

That's what happened at Sinai. Israel didn't stop worshiping, they just redirected it. They traded waiting for dancing. Trust for efficiency.

The delay is always deliberate. It's God's way of sifting the soul. It's calculated with divine precision by the God who exists outside of time. He knows just how many seconds need to tick on the clock before who we really are shows up. None of this is to shame or condemn us. It's to heal us. God already knows who we are. He wants *us* to see it, so the "old self" that's still trying to move into the next season can be buried in the soil of the in-between. The hallway can become the burial ground of who we used to be...if we can endure the delay.

Ishmael in the Hallway of Delay

The delicate space between God's word spoken and the promise fulfilled is sacred—and dangerous. It's the breeding ground for shortcuts that can affect generations.

Ishmael is always born in the hallway of delay.

I'll explain what I mean, but first, a little backstory.

In Genesis 15, God delivers a promise to Abraham...one so precious it would shift the course of history:

> "One who will come from your own body shall be your heir."[69]

Then He takes Abraham outside, points toward the stars, and says,

> "Look now toward heaven, and count the stars if you are able to number them... So shall your descendants be."[70]

It was a specific promise; sealed in blood and confirmed through a covenant ceremony where God Himself passed between the slaughtered halves of sacrifice, binding Himself to this powerful word.

---

69. Genesis 15:4
70. Genesis 15:5

The only problem, of course, was Sarah was barren. And both of them were well beyond the age to have children. But none of that mattered anymore, God had spoken!

Let's play the timeline game again: If you're Abraham, how long would you expect before Sarah becomes pregnant? A week or two? Perhaps we should give a month's grace period in the event that God had a lot on His plate?

Not sure about you, but if I get a word like this from God Himself, in an encounter complete with smoking pots and covenantal sacrifice, then you can bet your last dollar I'm searching name ideas. We're Googling stroller reviews. I'm figuring out if we should homeschool or trust God with the public school thing. I mean, why wait to fill out the baby registry (does registering at Nordstrom put too much pressure on friends and family?)? God showed up and gave us a promise! Come on, Sarah, it's date night, honey!

I'm sure Abraham must have been beside himself with excitement...and expectation.

But then...one month turned into six.

One year turned into four, then five, then nine.

And still. . .nothing but barrenness.

And when the delay stretches into years, it's easy to start questioning everything.

Did I hear God right?

Maybe I misunderstood?

Did I mess up somewhere?

Was any of that real?

The thing is, Abraham had learned to live with barrenness in the past. Sarah had *always* been barren. I'm sure it was hard, but after years of managing the disappointment month after month, it just became the way it was...like a faint ache in his heart that he learned to carry through life.

But after the encounter, after the promise, after the covenant, the *present* barrenness wasn't just painful. It must have been breathtakingly confusing.

Put yourself in that man of faith's shoes. What would you do when *ten years* after God spoke the promise, you still see no sign of life? What Abraham was wrestling with wasn't just the silence of delay. It was the hunger that the word of God had created in him (more on this in Chapter 11). When God speaks, it always creates an appetite for what used to seem impossible, but now seems just around the corner. And hunger that goes unsatisfied for too long will always look for something to feed on.

Enter Hagar from stage left.

When Delay Births Alternatives

Abraham wasn't the only character in this story. And you're not the only character in yours. We all have people around us who can grow weary in the delay: a spouse, a family member, a close friend, a pastor. Someone close to us will eventually, out of love *or* frustration, suggest an idea about how God may want to get us out of the in-between. Even faith-filled communities can offer shortcuts disguised as wisdom.

For Abraham, that someone was Sarah.

Just as weary of waiting as her husband, she approached him with an idea:

> "Now behold, the Lord has prevented me from bearing children. Please go in to my maid; perhaps I will obtain children through her."[71]

Maybe *this* is how God intends to fulfill His promise. Maybe He's waiting for *you* to take the next step.

To be fair, Abraham and Sarah weren't turning their back on God. They were just trying to help Him out. But given enough time, even the most misguided choices can be spiritualized. So Abraham did what seemed to make the most sense when the promise was delayed.

And it worked. Hagar conceived. Life was finally forming in a house where barrenness once reigned.

But what was born out of impatience wasn't a fulfillment of the promise. It was a complication. And that complication now had a life of its own. When we manufacture human solutions to divine delays, we don't inherit promises; we birth really messy situations that we're now responsible for. The hallway is where

71. Genesis 16:2

every promise stands on trial. It's either protected or compromised.

If only Abraham had waited a little longer.

If only Sarah had held hope a little tighter.

If only they had trusted that the God who spoke would bring the word to pass.

But that's the nature of the hallway: it tests faith to the breaking point.

Maybe you're living with a word from God that feels unbearably delayed. Maybe you've begun to wonder if you should make something happen. Maybe you're entertaining your own Hagar solution, not because you've stopped believing God, but because you can't see how His promise could possibly come to pass.

Can I encourage you?

The God who spoke the stars into existence is perfectly capable of fulfilling His word to you. His timing may feel slower than yours, but that's only because His plans are greater than yours. What you perceive as a slow pace is actually the tempo of His intentional goodness. God isn't just giving you the thing He promised. He's forming in you the kind of character that can *carry* the promise without being crushed by it.

Every promise comes with the weight of responsibility, and without the internal strength to bear it, what was intended to be a gift becomes a burden. The hallway of delay is where God builds the unseen infrastructure of patience, endurance, trust, testimony, and the many facets of Christ-like character that can hold what God wants to do in your life.

Quick fixes and smooth transitions won't mature us. Expecting them is like assuming muscle will grow just because you walked into the gym. Walking through the door is step one, but no one ever won a body-building competition because they looked at a set of dumbbells. Growth comes through resistance. There is a deliberate process of strengthening specific muscles that has to take place.

We all have spiritual muscles that God wants to strengthen before we move into the next season. The liminal space, with its calculated delay, is designed to do just that.

When the Promise Breaks Through

Years passed after the birth of Ishmael. Then, when Abraham was ninety-nine years old, God spoke again:

> "At the *appointed time* I will return to you, about this time next year, and *Sarah* shall have a son."[72]

Just as there is an appointed time for bamboo to break through soil, an appointed time for Moses to descend the mountain, there was an *appointed time* for Abraham and Sarah to finally hold the promise in their arms... together. And when that moment finally came, it was

72. Genesis 18:14

clear that the God who promises to do exceedingly beyond all we could ask or imagine is also the sovereign God of times, seasons, doors, and wombs.

Matthew Henry writes,

> "God has an appointed time for his appointed work, and will be sure to do the work when the time comes; it is not for us to anticipate his appointments, but to wait his time. And it is a great encouragement to wait with patience; though the promised favour be deferred long, it will come at last."[73]

The Freshly Spoken Word

Fast forward a couple of thousand years, and a similar promise came to a young girl in Nazareth,

> "Do not be afraid, Mary, for you have found favor with God. And behold, you will conceive in your womb and bring forth a Son."[74]

Like Abraham, Mary believed the word spoken to her. But the angel added a line that serves all of us very well if we can get a hold of it,

> "For with God nothing will be impossible."[75]

Great verse, right?

---

73. Matthew Henry, *Commentary on the Whole Bible*, Genesis 18:14.
74. Luke 1:30-31
75. Luke 1:37

Well, actually, it's a weak translation of an even *better* verse.

The literal translation should read something more like this,

> "No freshly spoken word of God will be without ability."[76]

The idea is this: every word God speaks carries within itself the power to perform itself.[77] The transformative power of the word isn't external, it's contained *within* the word itself. When God speaks, that word already carries the creative energy to bring itself to pass.

But here's the part a lot of us miss: the transformative power contained within the word is *potential* power.

Think of it like the bamboo seed: everything the seed needs to explode with life is already inside, but until the seed is received into the right environment, for the right amount of time, it remains dormant. The word of God works the same way. It's perfect and complete, but it will not override our unbelief or impatience.

While a natural seed is activated by soil, water, and the proper temperature, the seed of God's word is activated by our faith. And the span of time between

---

76. There are two words at the end of this sentence that are ignored in most modern translations, *pas rhēma*. *Pas* means all/every and *rhēma* means the spoken word. The literal, word-for-word translation of the sentence would be "For nothing unable for God all spoken word"
77. James echoes this when he writes, "Receive the word implanted, which is able to save your souls." (James 1:21)

the word spoken and the promise fulfilled, the *delay*, is the opportunity given to each of us to either activate that word by faith or neutralize it with unbelief, loss of interest, or efforts to fulfill it in our own strength.

Faith doesn't *make* God's word true; it releases what's already true into time and space.

This is what theologians call the *law of restriction:* the word remains restricted until faith activates it. Heaven waits for human agreement. God's word is not a winning lottery ticket to be cashed in; it's an invitation to believe by faith what cannot *yet* be seen.

Every promise that comes from God demands that we now believe about Him what *He* believes about Himself. And He believes so deeply in His ability to perform the word that He entrusts it to us.

The question is: do you? Even when that word is delayed?

The Gift of the Delay

Delay is never wasted in the hands of God. We may want doors to open quickly. We may want the promise fulfilled without the ache of waiting. But God wants something deeper.

He wants a people who don't just receive His promises, but who partner with Him in bringing them to pass.

Delay is where desire is tested.

Delay exposes what we worship.
Delay refines our motives.
Delay is where faith grows roots deep enough to hold the weight of answered prayers.

And that's where we're headed next.

CHAPTER 7

FAITH IN THE FAMINE

"It is better to be in Canaan in famine, in the will of God, than in Egypt with plenty, but out of it."

- F.B. MEYER

They said there was gold in the hills.

So he sold everything, left home, and went west with nothing but a pickaxe, a dream, and a borrowed map. Thomas believed God was leading him. Maybe He was. Maybe He still would've been…if only Thomas had stayed.

He found his spot and started digging. At first, it was exciting. Every shovel of dirt felt like a step toward the promise. This was going to be it. This was going to change everything.

But then the days got longer. And the gold didn't show. Thomas had marked a date in his mind. *"If I don't see something by this point, I'm done."* So, when the deadline came and went, he packed it all up and left. Sold the land to a guy down the road who was looking for a place to camp.

The lucky guy who bought it found gold three feet below the same spot Thomas stopped digging.

Three feet.

What Thomas thought was failure was just unfinished. And when the outcome didn't meet his due date, he walked away from the very thing that rightfully belonged to him.

I wonder how many of us do the same.

We pray for an open door… but we give it an expiration date. We obey, but we give our obedience a finish line. And when the waiting drags longer than expected, we assume God has moved on, or we must've missed it.

But what if the breakthrough was just three feet away?

It's not the hallway that disqualifies us from the next season, it's the story we start telling ourselves in the middle of it. We convince ourselves that a closed door means a dead end. And so we pivot. We move on. We try to help God out.

> "Let us not grow weary in doing good, for at the proper time we will reap a harvest if we do not give up."[78]

---

78. Galatians 6:9 (NIV)

Let's go deeper into the story of Abraham. But before we move forward, we need to rewind the tape to when God called him out of his homeland.

God was leading Abraham into a land He would show him; a land of promise, a land flowing with unseen possibilities. Abraham obeyed. He left everything familiar behind and, by faith, stepped into the unknown.

Genesis 12 picks up the story of Abraham reaching his destination.

Picture yourself in that moment. You just made the journey from modern-day Baghdad to Israel…on foot. You're 75 years old, walking with your 65-year-old spouse, over 1,000 miles because God said there would be a blessing waiting at the finish line. And finally, five months later, you arrive in the land He told you about.

> "Now there was a famine in the land..."[79]

Hold up. I'm sorry, what? God didn't say anything about a famine. He said things like *great nation* and *blessing*.[80]

Abraham had obeyed God…and found *famine*?

So not only does he need to manage the barrenness of his wife, but now he's also got to find a way to manage the barrenness of the land God called him to.

---

79. Genesis 12:10
80. See Genesis 12:1-3

Barrenness behind.

Barrenness in front.

Barrenness all around.

The door to his old life was closed.

The door to fruitfulness wasn't yet open.

Welcome to the hallway, Abraham.

God was taking his man through a school of testing and formation. He was introducing Abraham to one of His favorite places of consecration: the liminal space. We've all stood in that dustbowl of barrenness:

> The new job didn't pan out like you expected.
> The first year of marriage was tougher than the movies promised.
> The ministry assignment feels more like a struggle than a revival.
> The prodigal child, whose salvation you believed for, is still far from home.

The hallway between your "yes" and God's fulfillment of the promise can feel brutal.

And that's exactly where Abraham found himself when He arrived in Canaan.

The Pragmatic Detour

Rather than sitting in the tension of unmet expectations, Abraham made a decision:

> "So Abram went down to Egypt to dwell there, for the famine was severe in the land."[81]

There's no evidence in Scripture that God told Abraham to go to Egypt. It was a pragmatic decision made in the spirit of self-preservation. A decision based solely on getting out of the tragedy of famine he found in the land God *had* called him to.

But a detour down to Egypt is always more dangerous than it seems. Pharaoh is a false hope. Egypt always overpromises and underdelivers. The hard, dry ground of Canaan is where God intended Abraham to be, not the fertile fields of the Nile.

The problem wasn't that Egypt had food.

The problem was that God hadn't led Abraham there.

The Available Grace Where God Calls You

The grace of God isn't floating in the abstract. It's anchored in obedience; directly connected to both time and place. There was no grace waiting for Abraham in Egypt. The grace was in Canaan.

Let me do my best to back that one up.

I first heard this idea of "available grace" while bracing for a brutal international flight with three small children. It was 2013, and we were flying from the Middle East to the United States. An overnight flight of multiple

81. Genesis 12:10

legs, long layovers, and longer flight times. Lindsey was concerned because our nine-month-old was, well, *nine months old*. When she shared her concern with a friend, the friend said, "*You can't worry about that now. The grace isn't available yet, but it will be when you get there.*"

That stuck with us. And we've held onto that truth so many times since then.

We can't worry about future seasons, future decisions, future blessings, or future grace.

> "Do not worry about tomorrow; for tomorrow will look after itself."[82]

This was a lesson Corrie Ten Boom learned as a little girl. Once, when she began to worry about the future, her father asked her, "Corrie, when you and I go to Amsterdam, when do I give you your ticket?" "Why, just before we get on the train." "Exactly. And our wise Father in heaven knows when we're going to need things, too. Don't run out ahead of Him, Corrie."[83]

We can what-if our way out of so many opportunities. And just as equally, we can what-if our way *into* situations God never intended for us. We can imagine what might happen if we stay where God has placed us, and because there's no grace in those imaginations, we start moving in our own strength and calling it wisdom. That's what Abraham did. The famine in Canaan caused

---

82. Matthew 6:34
83. Corrie ten Boom, *The Hiding Place*, with John and Elizabeth Sherrill (New York: Chosen Books, 1971), p. 67.

him to reason his way out of the grace that was available there. God didn't lead Abraham to Canaan just to let him die of hunger. There was provision in that famine that no bread from Pharaoh's table could ever match.

> "I have a kind of food you know
> nothing about."[84]

But Abraham missed that opportunity of experiencing God's provision in the midst of famine (more on that in a minute).

Yes, God was merciful to Abraham in spite of his detour to Egypt. But that says more about the character of God's kindness than it does about the strategy of Abraham. The Scriptures teach us that God's paths, not ours, drip with abundance.[85] Abraham's trip to Egypt became a search and rescue mission. *Get that guy back on God's path before he makes any more mistakes.*

The Hidden Costs of Escaping the Hallway

On the surface, Abraham's detour looked successful. He survived the famine. He came back to Canaan alive…still carrying the promise of God in his heart.

But survival doesn't always mean success.

When Abraham left Egypt, he didn't leave empty-handed. He brought something with him:

---

84. John 4:32
85. Psalm 65:11

> "Now Sarai, Abram's wife, had borne him no children. And she had an Egyptian maidservant whose name was Hagar."[86]

It was on his detour to Egypt where Abraham and Sarah met Hagar. And Hagar—the Egyptian maid—became a ticking time bomb inside Abraham's house.

Years later, when weariness set in and faith grew thin, she became Plan B; the embodiment of compromise living under his own roof. She was the escape hatch in case of emergency.

When Abraham forced himself out of the hallway of famine, he placed himself in a scenario that was out of alignment with what God had intended for him. He made himself unnecessarily susceptible to situations he was not yet ready to handle. He was vulnerable in Egypt because he was out of season. Because he was a man out of season, he stepped out from under grace and brought home something God never intended him to carry. This is the danger of taking detours.

When We Force Our Way Forward

When we leave the hallway too early to "fix" our famine, not only do we step out of the grace God intends to define our lives, but we often pick up burdens we were never meant to carry. Abraham didn't just pick up Hagar in Egypt, he picked up the bad habit of protecting himself when his wife's presence put him in harm's way.

---

86. Genesis 16:1

He learned it was okay to dishonor bridal covenant when worldly kings became jealous.

This wasn't the only time, either. The exact same thing happened in Genesis 20. *Twice,* Abraham lied about his wife to save his own skin.

And that pattern didn't die with him. It was passed on to his children. Years later, when Isaac had a beautiful wife of his own, he faced an almost *identical* situation,

> "Now there was a famine in the land, besides the previous famine that had occurred in the days of Abraham. So Isaac went to Gerar, to Abimelech king of the Philistines…When the men of the place asked about his wife, he said, 'She is my sister,' for he was afraid to say, 'my wife,' thinking, 'the men of the place might kill me on account of Rebekah, since she is beautiful.'"[87]

Call it a normal cultural practice all you want, but lying about covenant when it looks like it will cost you is not kingdom practice. Abraham may have survived his detour to Egypt, but Egypt sure left a mark, a mark so deep it was passed on to the next generation.

These are some of the consequences of forcing ourselves out of the liminal space. There is great grace there for whatever God believes we can handle: famine, barren wombs, and everything in between. But that grace is an intended grace for the intended

87. Genesis 26:1, 7

space God has you. When we force our way out of the in-between, just like Abraham, we pick up things that don't belong to us:

Wounds.

Broken relationships.

Unnecessary struggles.

Bad habits that can become generational issues our children have to deal with.

Every time we take matters into our own hands in the waiting, we risk entangling ourselves with things that were never part of God's plan. The hallway is never just about where you're going. It's about what you're carrying when you get there.

"Just Do Something"

When I was young in the Lord, I received some bad advice. I asked my pastor a question many of us have wrestled with at one point or another: *How do I know God's will for my life? What do I do when I don't know what to do next?*

At that point in my walk, I was standing in my own hallway. The door to my old life was closed. The door to calling and purpose hadn't opened yet. I was willing to do anything for Jesus, go anywhere with Him...if only He would tell me what to do.

My pastor handed me a book: *Just Do Something*. The premise was simple: Since God is sovereign, you don't need to agonize over what to do. Just move. Just act. God will bless your movement, and His sovereign will is going to work itself out in your life.

Get going!

Come on, Sarah, let's just go down to Egypt.

Come on, Abraham, just go into my maidservant.

I love and honor that pastor to this day. But now, with the scars and wisdom of hindsight, I know that "just do something" is the siren song of the impatient soul. It's the carnal whisper that gives false hope to those stuck in the middle. It leads countless believers to rush out of the space God intends to form them in, and into seasons that stretch them beyond what they have the grace for. God isn't looking for action, He's looking for obedient faith that knows how to trust Him in famines.

One of the hardest things you'll ever do is stay where God has you when it feels like He's no longer there.

It will test every part of your soul.

It will challenge every practical instinct you have.

It will make you feel foolish.

It will make you question whether you heard God at all.

But staying in the place of obedience, especially when it feels barren, is what prepares you for the fruitfulness God intends to release later. The land of promise, even in famine, holds more blessing in its soil than the abundance of a thousand Egypts.

Famine Feeding Faith

There's a *deeper* question buried in this story of Abraham's famine, one I don't hear asked very often: *why was there a famine in the land God called His man to?*

What was God's intention in bringing Abraham to a land that wasn't bearing fruit? Was it just bad luck? Bad timing? No deeper meaning, it just is what it is?

I don't think so.

Could it be that God wasn't leading Abraham into a land to inherit, but into a land to *heal*?

Could it be that the barrenness of Canaan was the reason God sent Abraham there?

Maybe—just *maybe*—God was looking for a man with enough faith to stand in the middle of famine and call down blessing.

I believe God purposely brought Abraham to Canaan in the midst of a famine because He wanted an image bearer to represent Him in a land that was not living under the blessing of His grace. What if Abraham had looked at the famine and believed God enough to heal it?

I believe God wanted Abraham to be a living declaration that when God plants His people in barren places, those places don't stay barren for long.

And neither do barren wives.

> "In days of famine they will enjoy plenty."[88]

Is there barrenness in your community, your job, your family, your church? What if you being there isn't a mistake? What if the famine is part of the assignment?

Our God is a redeemer. He brings life to dead things. And the primary way He moves in creation is through His people.

Where God has you may feel like the barren fields of Canaan, but what if God doesn't have you there because the ground is ready?

What if He called you there to *make* it ready?

Dust Bowl Faith

Centuries later, God would tell similar stories through ordinary people facing their own dry ground. During the Dust Bowl years of the 1930's, most families in the Oklahoma Panhandle abandoned their farms in search of better conditions out west.

But Bill and Caroline Henderson chose to stay.

It was one of the worst environmental disasters in American history. But the Hendersons believed God had called them to that land, and they believed He hadn't

88. Psalm 37:19

changed His mind just because the crops had stopped growing.

They dug deeper wells.

They planted windbreak trees.

They learned new methods of soil conservation.

And they prayed.

Year after year, they watched dust storms roll in like judgment.

But they didn't quit.

Eventually, the rains returned. The land began to heal. And the fields they once wept over turned green again.

The Henderson's found life "three feet away" from where everyone else stopped.

Their patience didn't just restore a farm. It restored a region. The same soil that once cracked with dryness became some of the most fertile farmland in America.

Jesus calls His followers "the salt of the earth" and "the light of the world." Salt is needed where decay has set in. Light belongs where darkness lingers. And faithful endurance, not a creative exit plan, is needed when the place God has called you to is barren and dry.

If God called you into a place that feels barren, it's not because He misjudged the soil. It's because He intends to bring life there—*through you.*

> "Your people will rebuild the ancient ruins and will raise up the age-old foundations; you will be called Repairer of Broken Walls, Restorer of Streets with Dwellings."[89]

If you retreat to Egypt, you may find temporary provision…but you'll miss your assignment. Egypt may feed you for a season, but Canaan is where famine becomes a testimony.

89. Isaiah 58:12

CHAPTER 8

TRUST: THE STEP AFTER FAITH

"Trust in the LORD with all your heart and lean not on your own understanding; in all your ways acknowledge Him, and He shall direct your paths."

- Proverbs 3:5-6

Faith and trust are not the same thing. I'll prove it to you.

In the summer of 1859, thousands of spectators lined the cliffs of Niagara Falls, drawn by the promise of a spectacle. A French acrobat named Charles Blondin had announced he would walk across the massive, 1,100-foot-long gorge on a rope just two inches thick. With nothing but a balancing pole in his hands and the roaring waters beneath him, Blondin took the first step… of many.

But he didn't just cross once. He crossed again and again and again. He crossed blindfolded, on stilts, even carrying a stove and stopping mid-way to cook an omelet. With every successful attempt, the crowds grew louder. Nothing seemed impossible for the man.

Then came the moment no one expected.

Blondin brought out a small wheelbarrow and turned to the cheering throng. "Do you believe I can carry a man across in this?"

The crowd erupted, "Yes! You can do anything!"

Then he smiled and asked, "Who wants to go first?"

Silence.

They had faith he could do it. But no one *trusted* him enough to stake their life on it.

We know the feeling. We believe God can carry us. We believe He's good. We've even cheered for others when they've taken steps of radical faith.

But when it's our turn to get in the wheelbarrow, to let go of control and say yes to a season we can't see the details of, it's not faith that's tested.

It's trust.

This chapter isn't about whether you believe God is faithful. It's about what happens when the only way forward is climbing in the wheelbarrow.

The Way of Trust

Solomon's words in Proverbs 3 invite us into a way of life that is profoundly simple, and deeply challenging:

> "Trust in the LORD with all your heart and lean not on your own understanding; in all your ways acknowledge Him, and He will direct your paths."[90]

To trust in the Lord with all your heart means there's no fallback plan. No trust left in yourself. No leaning on your own logic.

Matthew Henry puts it this way, "Those who know themselves cannot but find their own understanding to be a broken reed, which, if they lean on, will certainly fail them."[91]

Trusting the Lord means more than believing He exists. It means refusing to rely on our own understanding to get through life, and especially through the hallway between seasons. It's choosing His guidance when ours makes more sense. When doors close and nothing adds up, trust is what carries us through.

Faith is the starting point. It believes without needing proof. As Hebrews tells us, "faith is the substance of things hoped for, the evidence of things not seen."[92] Faith

---

90. Proverbs 3:5–6
91. Matthew Henry, *Matthew Henry's Commentary on the Whole Bible: Complete and Unabridged in One Volume*. (Peabody: Hendrickson), 1994.
92. Hebrews 11:1

says, "I believe God is as good as Jesus says He is." Blessed are those who have not seen and yet still believe.[93]

But trust goes a step further. Trust says, "*Because* I've experienced His goodness, I will follow Him wherever He leads." Faith may have gotten you where you are, but trust will get you where you're going.

To put it another way, faith got Peter into the boat with Jesus. Trust got him onto the water.

Trust is the difference between believing anything is possible—and doing the impossible.

Trust is the confident act of placing all your weight on God because He has proven Himself faithful time and again. Faith says God can be trusted. Trust acts on it.

Trust isn't passive. It steps forward, even when it's trembling. It moves when God whispers. It obeys, not out of certainty, but out of assurance born from consistency. As James reminds us, faith without works is dead.[94] The "works" he speaks of are not acts of religious striving; they are the visible evidence of invisible trust, the irrational acts of obedience that only make sense because God is who He says He is.

Brennan Manning wrote, "Trust is our gift back to God, and He finds trust so enchanting that Jesus died for love of it."[95]

---

93. John 20:29
94. James 2:17
95. Brennan Manning, *Ruthless Trust: The Ragamuffin's Path to God* (New York: HarperCollins, 2000), 2.

Of course, trust isn't easy. In fact, in seasons of loss—unemployment, betrayal, grief, uncertainty—the soil is rich for distrust to grow. Manning writes, "It requires heroic courage to trust in the love of God no matter what happens to us."[96]

And yet, it's in those very moments that we are invited to trust more deeply.

Over time, something beautiful happens: faith and experience begin to mingle. Testimony piles on testimony. And something shifts.

Faith matures into trust; a deep, settled confidence that God will be to us tomorrow who He has been to us every day before.

Which brings us to a deeper truth: trust often begins where clarity ends.

The Gift of Letting Go

Brennan Manning tells the story of a man named John Kavanaugh, who spent three months working at Mother Teresa's "House of the Dying" in Calcutta. Kavanaugh was in a season of transition, searching for direction, desperate for clarity about how to spend the rest of his life.

On his first morning there, he met Mother Teresa. She greeted him warmly and asked, "And what can I do for you?"

96. Ibid, 4.

Kavanaugh replied, "Please pray for me."

"What do you want me to pray for?" she asked.

Kavanaugh, eager to have someone like Mother Teresa petition God on his behalf, asked her to pray that he would have clarity.

Mother Teresa shook her head. "No, I will not do that," she said gently. "Clarity is the last thing you are clinging to… and must let go of."

Kavanaugh, not about to let the moment pass, remarked how she always seemed to have the clarity he longed for. Mother Teresa laughed. "I have never had clarity," she said. "What I have had is trust. So I will pray that you trust God."

Manning draws out the heart of that exchange:

> "The faith that animates the Christian community is less a matter of believing in the existence of God than a practical trust in His loving care under whatever pressure. The stakes here are enormous, for I have not said in my heart, 'God exists,' until I have said, 'I trust you.' The first assertion is rational, abstract, a matter perhaps of natural theology, the mind laboring at its logic. The second is communion, bread on the tongue from an unseen hand."[97]

That's trust. Not as a theory, but as a lived reality. A daily placing of our lives into God's unseen hands.

---

97. Ibid, 6.

To trust God doesn't mean we graduate from walking by faith; it means we receive grace to keep walking… eyes fixed on what is unseen, even when what can be seen shouts louder. In the face of affliction, Paul's encouragement to the Corinthians was not to lose heart. Even when everything outward seemed to be wasting away, the unseen work of God was still forming something eternal within them. He concludes with this kingdom truth,

> "We don't look at the things which are seen, but at the things which are unseen. For the things which are seen are temporary, but the things which are not seen are eternal."[98]

It's tempting to believe that trust will eventually reward us with clarity to see, that if we hold on long enough the fog will lift and everything will make sense. But trust doesn't always clear the fog. Often, it simply gives us the courage to keep going through it.

The Pilot and the Blind Landing

A seasoned bush pilot in Alaska once told of the most terrifying flight of his life. Flying low through a fog bank, his instruments failed. Visibility dropped to zero. The horizon vanished. There was no sense of up or down, only disorienting gray.

Panic whispered, *Take control.*

But he remembered his training: *trust the tower.*

---

98. 2 Corinthians 4:18

He radioed for help and obeyed the voice on the other end, one instruction at a time:

> "Drop 200 feet."
> "Bank left three degrees."
> "Now glide."

He couldn't see anything, but he could hear instructions from someone who could. And that was enough.

When he finally broke through the fog and saw the runway beneath him, he wept. And when he landed, it wasn't understanding that got him there. It was trust.

Trusting God in a hallway season often looks like this. It's a steady obedience in the gray; moving forward without any rational explanation to justify the decision or guarantee the outcome. It's what Brennan Manning calls "a movement grounded in the presence and promise of God."[99]

That kind of trust doesn't wait for the fog to lift. It discerns the whisper of God in the present moment and dares to say:

> "Into Your hands, I commit my spirit.
> Into Your hands, I entrust my body and mind.
> Whatever You want of me, I want of me.
> Into Your heart, I entrust my heart.
> Unto You, I abandon myself completely."[100]

---

99. Manning, *Ruthless Trust*, 12.
100. Ibid, 11.

Trust on the Altar

There are two mountaintops in Scripture where the essence of trust is laid bare: one is Moriah, the other Golgotha. On both, a son is laid on the altar. On both, the Father's will leads to unspeakable cost. And on both, we see that trust is choosing to remain where God has you, knowing that trust is the bridge between sacrifice and resurrection.

Abraham's Mountain

By now, we've traced Abraham's journey through famine, delay, and detour…through every hallway God used to shape his faith. But here on Mount Moriah, that road of formation comes to its most difficult test. God had promised Abraham a son, and through that son, a nation; descendants more numerous than the stars. Isaac was the embodiment of everything God had said. He was the laughter in Sarah's arms, the tangible expression of God's faithfulness.

And then came the unthinkable:

> "Take your son, your only son, whom you love, and offer him…"[101]

No explanation. No reason. Just a command to get into the wheelbarrow.

Abraham rose early. He saddled his donkey. He gathered wood for the fire and a knife for the offering. And for

---

101. Genesis 22:2

three days, he walked in silence with the promise by his side.

When they reached the mountain, Abraham told his servants, "Stay here with the donkey…the boy and I will go over there to worship, and we will return.'"[102]

Worship. The first time the word ever appears in Scripture.

No music. No stage. No crowd. Just obedient surrender offered on a mountain to the Father who delights in hearts that trust Him.

What follows is one of the most haunting questions in all of Scripture:

> "Father… where is the lamb?"

Where *is* the lamb? How can there be worship if there's no sacrifice?

> "God will provide."

Abraham didn't know how.

He didn't know when.
But he knew *who* He was worshipping on
that mountain.

And that was enough.

---

102. Genesis 22:4-5

<u>Jesus's Mountain</u>

Centuries later, another Son would climb another hill with wood on His back. But this time, there would be no ram in the thicket.

He would be the Lamb.

Jesus walked up His mountain fully aware of who was leading Him there. In obedient trust, He walked to His altar knowing the full weight of what was coming. But there was too much trust in the Father's goodness to turn back, even when worship led straight to a cross.

Abraham walked up his hill believing God would provide. Jesus walked up knowing *He* would be the provision.

The Invitation to Trust

This is the invitation of liminal seasons. When every door behind you has closed, and every door ahead remains locked, the hallway becomes your place of pause, trust, and worship.

While we might prefer to trust *after* we have clarity, God-honoring trust knows He is as trustworthy as Jesus says He is.

This kind of trust can only be born when the knife is in your hand and everything you hoped for is on the altar, when every option is sealed behind closed doors that God Himself has closed. It's forged when the cup of surrender is at your lips and you choose to say, *even here, I trust You.*

"God will provide."
"Your will be done."

This is where faith ripens into trust.

CHAPTER 9

CLOUD BY DAY, FIRE BY NIGHT

"There is a way that seems right to a man, but its end is the way of death."

- Proverbs 14:12

The wagons creaked and strained against the cracked earth as the families pushed westward. They had set out from Independence, Missouri, like so many others, answering the siren call of California. The spring of 1846 was filled with so much promise: fertile valleys, rich soil, and a future in which their children's children could thrive.

The way was well known. The Oregon Trail had carried thousands before them, slow and sure across the vastness of the frontier. But a new rumor was spreading among the pilgrims that year: a shortcut. A quicker path.

It was known as the Hastings Cutoff. A route that promised a faster arrival.

It was untested.

It was dangerous.

But the hope of shaving weeks off the journey from where they were to where they were going shouted louder.

The decision was made. The Donner Party turned from the established trail and followed a path of their own making.

They crossed salt flats that blistered their oxen's hooves. They moved through mountains hit by unseasonably early snow. Supplies dwindled. Their fate was sealed. And by the time the first rescue party broke through the winter drifts five months later, the California dream had frozen into a nightmare.

Forty-six men, women, and children were buried in the Sierra Mountains that year. But the truth is, they died long before the snow ever fell. They died the moment they chose the path that just seemed better.

When we find ourselves in the liminal space, the temptation is the same: find a shortcut.

But God didn't close the door on your previous season just to watch you force your way into the next. The God that brought you *to* the hallway is the same God who intends to lead you *through* it. But not before He forms something in you.

And one of those things is learning how to follow.

When the Cloud Stays Still

When Israel journeyed through the wilderness, they, too, were faced with a choice: move at God's command, or move on their own.

> "Now on the day that the tabernacle was raised up, the cloud covered the tabernacle; from evening until morning it was above the tabernacle like the appearance of fire. So it was always: the cloud covered it by day, and the appearance of fire by night...Whether the cloud remained above the tabernacle for two days, a month, or a year, the children of Israel would remain encamped and not journey; but when it was taken up, they would journey. At the command of the LORD they remained encamped, and at the command of the LORD they journeyed."[103]

Cloud by day. Fire by night.

Visible. Tangible. Divine.

There would be no shortcuts across the desert, only the slow obedience of following God's presence.

The story of Israel following the cloud by day and fire by night reminds us that God intentionally leads His people from one season to another. It's not in the Bible so that we marvel at what God did in a previous generation; it's

103. Numbers 9:15-16; 22–23

there to teach us that He intends to lead us the same way: faithfully, precisely, and at His pace.

Leading is His responsibility. Following is ours. Navigating closed doors and shifting seasons is never an issue of God's ability to lead. It's an issue of our willingness to follow.

When doors close and seasons shift, it's vital to recognize *how* God is leading so we can see *where* He's leading. On the surface, it seems Israel had an advantage. They could see the divine cloud lift and move. They knew to pack their tents and follow.

But just because Israel could see something physical doesn't mean they had it easier. We have something better.

We have the leading of the Spirit.

And for people of the Spirit, we can trust that God is really good at leading those who are really good at going the wrong direction.

Blocked Paths and Closed Doors

Picture it: you're a missionary. You want to visit churches where the gospel is still taking root. Saplings are fragile, so you set out on your journey convinced that God would, *of course*, want to strengthen the faith of these new believers and, *of course*, preach the gospel to increase their numbers.

This is good. It's right.

It's the sacred work of the gospel.

But even holy intentions are no substitute for divine direction.

This was the situation Paul and his missionary team found themselves in.

Luke tells us plainly,

> "They were forbidden by the Holy Spirit to preach the word in Asia...They tried to go into Bithynia, but the Spirit of Jesus did not permit them."[104]

How could the good thing not be the *God* thing?

Paul wasn't some reckless zealot chasing spiritual thrills. He wasn't moving in selfish ambition as he set out to *preach the gospel* in Asia. He was walking in obedience to the ministry Jesus Himself had entrusted to him. And still, the answer was a closed door.

Scripture doesn't give us the details, but I have to wonder if Paul was confused. Was he frustrated that doors were closing with no explanation? Was this why he later wrote to the Colossians to "pray for us, that God may open a door for our message"?[105]

People all around him were dying in their sin, and Paul had the medicine. Time was short. So why would Jesus close the door on the very work He had called Paul to do? Closed doors are the enemy's strategy, right...not

104. Acts 16:6, 7

105. Colossians 4:3

God's? Did Paul rebuke the devil? Surely Paul rebuked the devil. Maybe he forgot to bind him?

No.

There was no binding

No rebuking.

Just waiting.

Listening.

And I imagine praying…lots of praying.

Then…breakthrough.

> "A vision appeared to Paul in the night. A man of Macedonia stood and pleaded with him, saying, 'Come over to Macedonia and help us.'"[106]

The cloud had moved. The direction became clear.

> "Immediately we sought to go to Macedonia, concluding that the Lord had called us to preach the gospel to them."[107]

Now Paul could confidently move forward *with* God. Not with good ideas, not with urgent need or opportunity, but with Presence. The unmistakable hand of God leading him on the right path.

The fruit of Paul recognizing a closed door for what it was, and realizing the cloud was moving in a direction he

---

106. Acts 16:9 - Macedonia is modern-day Southeastern Europe
107. Acts 16:10

didn't expect, had multigenerational impact that touches you and me to this day.

You see, not only was the gospel proclaimed and churches planted on that redirected journey, but it was there—in Macedonia—that Paul saw the gospel take root in cities we know well: Philippi, Thessalonica, Corinth, Ephesus, Galatia.

Have you ever been blessed by the words of, say, 1 Corinthians or Galatians? What about Philippians? Ephesians? That's right, we have at least *seven* books of the Bible because Paul knew what to do with closed doors.[108]

Righteousness had gone before him, making God's footsteps his pathway. That's the promise of Psalm 85:13,

> "Righteousness goes before him and makes His footsteps our pathway."

And obediently following the cloud always results in fruit:

> "*Your* paths drip with abundance."[109]

Paul knew what to do with closed doors. Nothing... nothing but wait for the cloud to move, and follow wherever it led.

My Own Macedonia Call

---

108. Philippians, 1 & 2 Thessalonians, Ephesians, 1 & 2 Corinthians, & Galatians

109. Psalm 65:11

Paul's story reminds me of a moment in my own life when God's direction didn't look the way I thought it would.

I was traveling through Africa, scheduled to spend a few days in Kenya before driving across the border to Tanzania.

On my third day in Kenya, I woke up with an uneasy feeling about crossing the border. It was odd; up to that point, I'd been *more* excited about the Tanzania leg of my trip. But I couldn't shake the unrest in my spirit. The best way to describe it was a lack of peace.

It reminded me of Paul's situation described in 2 Corinthians 2:12-13,

> "When I came to Troas to preach Christ's gospel, and a door was opened to me by the Lord, I had no rest in my spirit..."

That afternoon, one hour before we were scheduled to leave for Tanzania, I told the Kenyan brothers traveling with me that we needed to pause long enough to seek the Lord together. We agreed to meet at my hotel the next morning for prayer.

When we gathered in my room the next morning, I shared with them the story from 2 Corinthians 2, how Paul felt unrest even though the Lord had opened a door for him. Not every open door is meant to be walked through. Sometimes God opens doors to *test* what's leading us (more on that in Chapter 14).

But there was hope in the next verse:

> "But thanks be to God, who always leads us in triumph in Christ, and through us reveals the fragrance of the knowledge of Him in every place."[110]

I also shared the story of Paul's Macedonian call in Acts 16.

With those two passages of Scripture anchoring our faith, we began to pray.

After about forty-five minutes, I asked if anyone sensed something from the Lord…perhaps a prophetic word, a vision, a Scripture. Mesh, a man with an incredibly authentic and disciplined prayer life, said,

> "After we prayed for about ten minutes, I saw a vision. We were standing on a stone mountain. A door was opened for us that led up to a high place of prayer. I heard Obadiah 1:17, 'On Mount Zion there shall be deliverance. And the house of Jacob will possess their inheritance.'"

Interestingly, Mesh was sitting next to a man named Jacob. And Jacob had recently purchased sixty-three acres of land…*at the base* of the stone mountain Mesh saw in his vision.

As we were marveling at that connection, Jacob's phone rang. It was someone from the village where his land is

110. 2 Corinthians 2:14

located. We half-joked that it was our own *Macedonian call.*

Then, as if to confirm it all, my father, who had woken up at 2 a.m. to pray for us in real time, sent me a text message. It read:

> "Don't know if this means anything, but I keep getting an emphasis on the number 7."

The stone mountain that Mesh saw in his vision—the one on Jacob's land—the locals call that area The *Seven* Elephants.

Thanks be to God who always leads us in triumph!

We made plans to visit the village of the Seven Elephants the next day. What happened there became a turning point, not just for me, but for our whole church community. It's now our base of operations in Africa.

That very week we began digging a water well there that turned out to be the most abundant and clean well our team has ever dug. I was also able to spontaneously meet with thirty-three local pastors who shared their vision for the region and how we could partner with them to transform their communities with the gospel. Three months later, a team of pastors from our church in California returned to teach and pour into eighty more regional pastors surrounding the Seven Elephants.

A door of opportunity had flung wide open…born not from striving, but from *stopping*. From refusing to force our way down a path God didn't intend us to be on.

Elijah and the Still Small Voice

The prophet Elijah knew something about redirection, too.

After Elijah's showdown on Mount Carmel—after fire fell from heaven, after false altars were consumed, after the enemies of God were defeated—you would think he would be riding high on faith. But instead, Elijah ran for his life.

> "And there he went into a cave…and the word of the Lord came to him, 'What are you doing here, Elijah?'"[111]

Some may say that God led Elijah there. I don't think so. I believe Elijah followed the wrong cloud to that cave; the cloud of his own fear, disappointment, and unmet expectations. Jezebel was after his life, the nation hadn't turned back to God as he had hoped, and he believed it was just a matter of time before he ended up like all the other prophets: dead and forgotten.

And then came the test: would Elijah keep following the cloud of fear, or return to the cloud of God's presence?

> "Then He said, 'Go out, and stand on the mountain before the LORD.'

111. 1 Kings 19:9

> And behold, the LORD passed by, and a great and strong wind tore into the mountains and broke the rocks in pieces before the LORD, but the LORD was not *in* the wind;
> and after the wind an earthquake, but the LORD was not *in* the earthquake;
> and after the earthquake a fire, but the LORD was not *in* the fire;
> and after the fire a still small voice."[112]

A still. Small. Voice.

Elijah knew how to find God in the fire. But did he know how to follow the whisper?

It was in that whisper that God gave Elijah his next assignment. But first, He repeats the question,

> "What are you doing here, Elijah?

Has God ever found you in a cave?

Have you ever run from a season, convinced it was going to kill you?

Have you ever thought that you were the only one still standing for righteousness and truth, only to find yourself hiding in a place God never asked you to go?

Maybe you haven't heard the whisper yet—but He's still asking:

---

112. 1 Kings 19:11–12

> What are you doing here? I didn't lead you here. My people are not cave dwellers; they mount up on wings like eagles and soar to heights of My making.

God confronted Elijah with the reality of where he was. He doesn't shame Elijah for the wrong turn; He simply calls him back to the right path.

> "Go…return on your way."[113]

In other words: *Go back to where you took the wrong turn and follow Me again. You're somewhere I never sent you, but that's okay. Let's dust you off and walk together again.*

If you've taken a wrong turn, let Elijah's story give you hope. God's grace is never so fragile it can't chase you down. His voice is never so faint He can't call you in your cave. His eyes are not so dim they can't find you in your hiding spot.

He is the Good Shepherd who knows how to lead His sheep. No wrong turn is wrong enough to lose you. If fear led you there, it's okay. If rebellion led you there, it's okay. If disappointment led you there, it's okay. Whatever brought you into the cave, you can trust He knows how to lead you out of it.

Verse 13 paints a beautiful close to the story,

> "Elijah wrapped his face in his cloak and went out of the cave and stood in the entrance of the cave."

---

113. 1 Kings 19:15

The word *cloak* literally means splendor, glory, and mantle. Elijah didn't just grab a coat to keep warm. He wrapped himself in the calling God had never taken away.

Which means his wrong turn didn't disqualify him.

And neither does yours.

If you've made mistakes, hear this: you are not disqualified from carrying the glory God intends to wrap you in. He knows your frame. Even when you run—like Jonah, like Elijah—you're not disqualified. There is still a splendor He intends to weave into your life. By faith, wrap yourself again in what He gave you. Take your stand at the entrance of whatever cave you've been hiding in, and look for the cloud of His presence to lead you.[114]

Final Reflections

The story of the Donner Party, the journey of Israel through the wilderness, Paul's blocked paths, and Elijah's cave all reveal different responses to closed doors. Yet each bears the same warning…and the same promise:

---

114. We are living in a day where church leaders believe it's acceptable to remain in positions of authority even after unrepentant sin that wounded others has been exposed in their lives. What I am offering as encouragement in this section is not that. Following your own ideas or letting fear keep you from God's direction is not the same as hurting others through moral failure or abuse of power. God's grace is limitless, and the blood of Jesus covers all sin, but Scripture is clear: there are sins that disqualify a person from leading God's people. Forgiveness restores fellowship, but it does not automatically restore leadership.

You were never meant to lead yourself.

You were always meant to be led by God.

And if you allow Him, He will.

The delicate space between seasons is never navigated by ambition, good ideas, or fear.

It can only be crossed by trusting the steady, faithful leading of a God who knows the way…even when we don't.

Sometimes the cloud of God's leading moves quickly. Other times, it lingers. And even when everything in us aches to move, we must learn to stay still too.

The Donner Party shows us that not every shortcut is a gift.

Paul reminds us that not every open door is from God.

Elijah teaches us that wrong turns don't mean disqualification.

And Israel's story shows us that not every wilderness is wasted.

God is not asking you to create the way. He's not even asking you to *understand* the way. He's asking you to follow Him.

If you've taken a wrong turn, hear this: His grace is sufficient to lead you home.

If you're waiting for the next step, hear this: His cloud will lift when the time is right.

And if you're standing at the entrance of your cave, wondering if the calling still rests upon you, hear this: wrap yourself again in His splendor, lift your eyes toward the horizon, and be ready to follow Him again.

The cloud doesn't stay still forever. There comes a moment when the same Presence that held you begins to move again—sometimes faster, sometimes farther than you expected. And when it does, everything familiar starts to feel different.

In the next chapter, we'll explore what happens when God begins to move ahead.

CHAPTER 10

THE TENSION OF THE THREE-DAY JOURNEY

"I have been driven many times upon my knees by the overwhelming conviction that I had nowhere else to go."

- Abraham Lincoln

The year was 1861.

A cold March wind swept through Washington, D.C., as Abraham Lincoln raised his hand and took the oath of office. The applause was polite but thin. Eleven Southern states had already seceded. The Union was unraveling thread by thread. What should have been the pinnacle of his political career felt more like standing on the edge of national collapse.

The newly elected President was a man of conviction, but heaven offered little clarity for the path ahead. Revelation lagged behind responsibility. The White House itself had the feel of a tomb—curtains drawn, windows cracked, the sound of distant gunfire echoing across the Potomac. His closest advisors argued constantly. His generals disobeyed orders or refused to act. Even his wife, Mary, was sinking into grief and emotional turmoil after the death of their son Willie.

In his letters, Lincoln confessed that he could not see a way forward. "My own wisdom," he wrote, "seems insufficient." He would often pace the halls alone long after midnight, praying softly under his breath. One aide described entering the room and finding him on his knees, face in his hands, pleading for light enough just to take the next step.

He was a man called by God to hold a fractured nation together, yet the grace to do so seemed to have gone ahead of them all. He bore the weight of a thousand decisions and the loneliness of command. When he finally issued the Emancipation Proclamation on January 1, 1863, it was from a place of trembling faith. "I made a solemn vow before God," he later said, "that if He gave us the victory at Antietam, I would consider it a sign to free the slaves." The battle had been bloody and uncertain, but he kept his vow.

And still, peace didn't come. The war dragged on for two more years. The nation's wounds deepened. He waited in the tension between what He believed God was doing in this new nation and what his eyes could see unraveling all around him.

Lincoln lived in the hallway between war and peace. He was learning the hardest kind of obedience: trusting that grace hadn't left, it was simply waiting for him beyond the horizon.

History now sees the fruit of that man's obedience, but in real time, it was agony. So many prayers unanswered. Headlines heaping accusation upon accusation. Every day a lesson in walking without sight.

The Tension of the Three-Day Journey

Our family once found ourselves living in a space that no longer carried the grace it once did. Like Lincoln, we were caught between grace lifted and grace revealed.

It was 2020. The confusion of life under COVID restrictions seemed to occupy everyone's attention. Everyone, that is, except for our family. We were in the middle of a delicate transition—from the foreign mission field where we had faithfully served God, to wherever He was leading us next. The world may have been arguing about face masks, but we were trying to figure out what in the world God was thinking...and was Covid really the reason we began to feel out of place in the land we had grown to love?

During this season of uncertainty, the Lord drew me to a small, easily overlooked passage in the book of Numbers. On the surface, it seemed like a simple record of Israel's journey through the wilderness. But underneath it was a lesson that marked our family.

I call it *the tension of the three-day journey.*

> "The ark of the covenant went before them a three days' journey, to search out a resting place for them." (Numbers 10:33)

Can you picture it? The ever-present cloud of God's glory hovering over the camp, the visible assurance that He was with His people, suddenly lifts. Trumpets sound. A hush descends over the camp as two million people watch the presence of God move ahead toward the horizon.

Hurry, chase after it!

Not so fast.

Before Israel could move, God had to go ahead… searching out a new place of rest.

The grace, so to speak, lifted.[115]

Have you ever felt a season coming to an end, when the grace that once made that place a delight is just, well, gone? The meetings feel heavier. The conversations drain you. The joy that once overflowed now trickles like water from a cracked well.

That's the tension of the three-day journey.

That's the delicate space between two breaths.

It's in that fragile moment, when it feels like separation, that God is actually preparing a resting place in your *next*

115. This is confirmed in Deuteronomy 1:33, "The Lord your God went in the way before you to search out a place for you...to show you the way you should go...fire by night, cloud by day."

season. He hasn't abandoned you. He's just gone ahead of you.

I remember how it felt when we were living in that in-between...navigating the tension of our own three-day journey. The things I had once loved—the prayer meetings, the discipleship classes, the ministry rhythms that gave shape to my days—suddenly felt unusually difficult. The motivation for what had once been so life-giving was gone. Not because I loved the people I was serving any less, but because the grace to do what I'd been doing had lifted and gone ahead.

It's here, in the tension of the three-day journey, that many believers lose their way. It's where we can lose faith, become confused, and begin to doubt.

It was in the tension of his own three-day journey that Job's friends filled the confusion with accusation: *perhaps you've sinned, and God's back is turned in judgment*? In the three-day journey, Samson confided in Delilah, Esau sold his birthright for a bowl of chili, and Moses killed an Egyptian.

The dreams of many well-intentioned saints are buried in the wilderness of the three-day journey, simply because they couldn't survive the tension of grace lifting and going ahead to prepare what was next.

When Grace Lifts

It will be uncomfortable when God closes the door on a season He no longer intends for you to be in. That's by design. You're being weaned off what once fed you. And the goal is not for God to now gently coax you along in hopes of making your journey as comfortable as possible. The purpose now is for you to see what He sees: the place that had grown so comfortable has become too small for who you're becoming. The grace lifting is His goodness pulling you forward.

Our inheritance of glory to glory is not a horizontal move.[116] It's vertical. Ever been climbing? Then you know that moving upward makes demands on the entire person. It requires strength, focus, courage, and faith in the rock you're resting your weight on when everything in you just wants to sit down.

To ascend into the measure of glory God intends for you will make similar demands. Vertical movements are always violent. Comfort doesn't climb, it rolls over and goes back to sleep.

> "While his men slept, his enemy came and sowed tares."[117]

Comfort waits for the cloud to come back.

Thomas Watson, the 17th-century Puritan preacher, writes in *Heaven Taken By Storm*,

> "The motion toward heaven is violent.[118] The stone moves easily to the center; it has an innate propensity downward, but to draw up a millstone into the air is done by violence because it is against nature. So to lift up the heart to heaven

116. See 1 Corinthians 4:18
117. Matthew 13:25
118. Matthew 11:12

> in duty is done by violence, and we must provoke ourselves to it."[119]

Even now, as I write this in the workshop behind our house, there's a nest of baby birds over the door. I hear them chirping every time their mother returns with food. They're comfortable. Their needs are met. They're safe.

But at some point very soon, they'll be pushed.

That nest will no longer be a home that can sustain them. To stay would mean starvation. They were never meant to die full in the nest—they were meant to live hungry in the sky.

The grace lifting from a season God no longer intends for you is designed to unsettle you. That restlessness you feel, that subtle agitation in what used to feel like home, it might not be a problem to fix. It might just be heaven's way of pushing you forward.

Another Three-Day Journey

It's one thing to imagine Israel in the wilderness watching the cloud lift. It's another to imagine the disciples staring at a sealed tomb in Jerusalem, wondering whether God has left... forever.

All of their hope rested in *that* Man now resting in *that* tomb.

They believed.

---

119. Thomas Watson, *Heaven Taken By Storm* (The Northampton Press, Orlando Fl., 2007), pg. 14.

They left everything.

They followed.

And now, He was gone.

The One who called Himself the Resurrection and the Life was now buried in a borrowed tomb. The One who raised the dead was now sealed behind the closed doors of death.

What's to stop those who killed Hope from coming for those who had hoped in Him?

It was a three-day journey of fearful silence for the disciples.

A three-day journey of grace lifted.

A three-day journey of haunting questions and the collapse of everything they thought they knew.

It was a closed door unlike any other. And the stone rolled against the tomb of their Messiah seemed like a cruel period at the end of a beautiful sentence.

I imagine that particular Sabbath was the stillest in history, at least on the surface. Outwardly, Jerusalem slept. Underneath the stillness, the followers of Jesus were paralyzed by grief and fear. It must have felt as though Jesus took every trace of His peace with Him. It's fitting that all four Gospels are silent about that day. Nothing was happening because everything had died.

Where does God go when it seems He's no longer with you?

Who can say, except for that tomb on the edge of town?

But the tomb wasn't the end. It was just a passageway—an unexpected door to the resting place God was preparing for us all.

Jesus went ahead of us on the ultimate three-day journey. He descended into death itself, seized the keys from its grasp, made a public spectacle of every enemy, disarmed every power that once held humanity captive,[120] and tore down the dividing wall that divided us all from Him.

On the surface, that Sabbath looked still.

But *underneath*—it was seismic.

And in His rising, our resting place was fully prepared: in the age to come, and even now, in our own sacred space between seasons. Jesus has gone ahead of us, preparing a place of confident rest for the tension of our own three-day journeys.

Choosing How to Wait

The three-day journey will come to each of us, sooner or later. And when it does, we'll have a buffet of choices laid before us as to how we wait.

---

120. See Colossians 2:15

We can wait like Thomas, the wounded skeptic, who said he wouldn't believe again unless he could thrust his hand into the wounds of Jesus. His pain of misplaced hope hardened into a paralysis of unbelief.

Or we can wait like the two disciples on the road to Emmaus, who, when the story didn't unfold as they expected, turned their backs on Jerusalem and left. Disappointment became their compass, and they decided *they* would chart their course from now on.

Or we can wait like Mary Magdalene; crushed, grieving, but faithful. She came to the tomb carrying spices for the body of the One she loved. She came in mourning, yes, but she also came in worship. She refused to let her disappointment steal her devotion. And it was Mary—not Peter, not John, not Thomas—who first heard the resurrected King call her name.

Doubt. Fear. A resolve to never be fooled again.

Or worship.

In the tension of the three-day journey, we all get to choose how we wait.

The three-day journey is not just about what God is doing on the other side.

It's about what we are allowing Him to do on the inside while we wait for Him.

Am I suggesting there's no grace for the hallway? Of course not. A new grace is present for those moments of delay. The problem is, we get so used to the grace of the *last* season that we don't recognize the grace for the in-between. We try to live today's assignment with yesterday's anointing.

And that's why men like Saul, Esau, Moses, and Abraham—men who knew God's voice—made devastating decisions in the tension of transition.

The confusion that comes with shifting seasons is normal. The swirl of thoughts and emotions is part of the journey. But if we can name what's happening, if we can recognize that the cloud of grace has gone ahead us—and this is something God is doing for our good—we can posture ourselves like Mary:

Worshipful.

Hopeful.

Ready for whatever comes next.

CHAPTER 11

THE ROOM WITH NO WINDOWS

"When you pray, go into your room, close the door, and pray to your Father who sees in secret..."

- Matthew 6:6

Some things only grow in hidden places.

We tend to see closed doors as denials: jobs that didn't open up, dreams delayed, clarity that never came. But Jesus saw them differently.

In Matthew 6:6, He invited His followers to embrace the closed door. To make it part of their rhythm with Him. But Jesus didn't say *if* you find yourself behind a closed door, He said *when*:

"When you pray…close the door, and pray to your Father who sees in secret…"[121]

121. Matthew 6:6

The closed door is as central to walking with Jesus as any other promise of the gospel. Yet, like most things in His kingdom, it's rarely what our flesh wants.

We want the open spaces, the panoramic views, and clear direction. But intimate things are inappropriate for those public spaces. Certain covenantal things only happen behind closed doors. To bring them into the public makes them common.

Some things are so sacred, they require closed doors.

In one of our families in-between seasons, the Lord showed us the value of the closed door. We had said yes to the next season, but the next season hadn't said yes to us. We had just left the Middle East, moved by a flurry of leading from the Lord that our assignment in Iraq was complete. We knew God was calling us to California, but we didn't yet know *where* in California. So we stayed with Lindsey's parents in North Carolina...and waited in the hallway.

It was the week of Thanksgiving when we arrived in North Carolina. There was no welcome packet. No detailed plan. Just closed doors...and enough faith to believe God hadn't forgotten us.

All we could do was pray. And pray. And pray.

We fasted as a family on Wednesdays. We talked about the transition with our kids, hoping to help them learn about the liminal space. We strengthened our faith with stories from Scripture of God's faithfulness in leading His people.

And did I mention we prayed?

Some of our prayers were faith-filled mountain movers. Others were laced with doubt and frustration. All the while, the doors around us remained closed. Jesus said to go behind those closed doors and pray. So we did.

At times, it felt like there was no oxygen in the hallway. Like our family's identity had been snuffed out. If we weren't missionaries in Iraq, then who were we? We couldn't go back, and nothing was opening ahead.

But day after day, the altars we built in that liminal space became like sacred spaces in time.

Prayer became our oxygen.

Many mornings, the Lord woke me up at 3:30, inviting me to the secret place. I'd slip out of bed and meet Him in the stillness. I prayed the Word. I prayed in the Spirit. I prayed exhausted. I prayed without ceasing.

Those closed doors were a personal invitation from the Father to take our seat in the secret place.

> "You called in trouble, and I delivered you; I answered you in the secret place of thunder."[122]

---

122. Psalm 81:7

That liminal space became our secret place of thunder. And in due time God answered...like He always does.

And now, as I write these words at my dining table in California, deep into the season we had once only prayed for, I find myself missing the simplicity of that hemmed-in space. Fasting together as a family. Crying out to God in the tension of mystery and possibility. The shared expectancy. The long, slow mornings of prayer where the slightest whisper felt like a clue from heaven.

It was an adventure behind closed doors.

Our hidden season was holy, but it wasn't unique. Others have walked into far deeper silence and come out shining.

That's the gift that the hallway offers us, an opportunity to scale back the things in life that present themselves as overly valuable. And when you find yourself in survival mode—and the hallway often feels like that—only the bare necessities remain. Spiritual habits that get neglected in the hustle of life become the mode of survival in the liminal space. Prayer becomes valuable again. Seeking God in the early hours of the day becomes foundational. Fasting becomes essential. The frivolous ways we spend our resources become exposed. The pressure of the hemmed-in season can squeeze out the fundamentals of our faith,

> "When you give…when you pray…when you fast."[123]

---

123. Matthew 6:2, 6, 16

There is an understanding that following Jesus includes these rhythms in our walk. Jesus says it's how we "practice our righteousness."[124] When the doors are closed around us, we have the opportunity to practice being who we really are for an audience of One.

The Sacred Secret Place

Richard Wurmbrand knew a thing or two about practicing his righteousness behind closed doors. On Sunday morning, February 29, 1948, Wurmbrand, a Romanian pastor, was walking to church as he did every Sunday. A van pulled beside him. Two men jumped out, shoved him inside, and drove off. He was thrown in prison for what would eventually be fourteen years.

His name was erased. His identity was hidden. Government agents, posing as former prisoners, told Wurmbrand's wife they had seen his funeral.

Richard Wurmbrand ceased to exist in the public space.

He was a captive man locked behind the doors of torture and psychological warfare. His captors weren't content to break his body, they wanted to dismantle his mind. For seventeen hours a day, propaganda recordings echoed through his cell:

> "Communism is good. Christianity is stupid. Give up. Give up."

Lies on repeat. Day after day. Hour after hour.

---

124. Matthew 6:1

The goal wasn't just to punish the pastor. The communists wanted to reprogram him.

And that was just the beginning. His body was carved, burned, and beaten. His bones were broken.

He spent the first three years in solitary confinement; twelve feet underground, in a cell with no windows, no light, no sound, and no concept of time. The walls were padded. The guards wore felt on their shoes just to heighten the torture of silence.

The isolation was so intense that many prisoners lost their minds within weeks.

But Wurmbrand made a decision. Every day, he would compose a sermon in his mind, deliver it out loud to the darkness, and offer it to the Lord as worship.

He later said those sermons were his lifeline. "I had no Bible," he wrote, "but the words I had hidden in my heart became like manna."

No pulpit. No audience. No altar calls. Just a man alone with God behind a closed door. The same door that locked him away from the world locked him in with God.

And did I mention that Wurmbrand prayed in his secret place? Oh, he prayed.

He built an altar of prayer in that underground cell and transformed every inch of those 144 square feet into a secret place of thunder.

He prayed for his captors. He prayed for the nations. For his family. For anything and everything. Solitary confinement may have hemmed Wurmbrand in, but it didn't hem in his prayers. No wall could stop his intercession from reaching the Father who sees in secret.

In 1964, Wurmbrand was released with a $10,000 ransom paid to the Romanian Communist regime by the Norwegian branch of the Mission to the Jews.

Years later, when he looked back on his season of mind-numbing isolation from the comfort of his freedom, Wurmbrand said,

> "I suffered, but I had the presence of Jesus with me in such a real way. I would not exchange that time for anything—not even a palace."[125]

I would not exchange that time for anything.

Carole C. Carlson wrote in her biography of Wurmbrand, *In the Shadow of the Cross*, that after moving to the West, Wurmbrand often struggled to maintain that same level of intimacy with God. The distractions of freedom, comfort, and ministry demands made it hard to find what he had once known so vividly in the underground. He missed the purity. The immediacy. The sense that there was nothing, *nothing,* between him and Christ.

Wurmbrand recalled how he and his fellow prisoners would sometimes dance in their cells,

---

125. Richard Wurmbrand, *Tortured for Christ* (Bartlesville, OK: Living Sacrifice Book Co., 1967), p. 44.

> "We were terribly hungry, beaten, and tortured. But we had forgotten all of this when we felt the presence of the Holy Spirit. I can't describe the joy in the cell. Sometimes we were so joyful, we felt we would burst if we didn't express it. We did not know on which day of the week or which hour of the day it was, but it didn't matter. The Holy Spirit was with us."[126]

He never glamorized suffering. But he did refuse to ignore what it had given him: unfiltered access to Jesus. It became a sacred place. He had been to the darkest, most isolated, and secret space and found Christ to be enough...*more* than enough.

> "I have found truly joyful Christians only in the Bible, in the Underground Church, and in prison."[127]

The Reward of the Secret Place

Jesus didn't say *if* you pray, but *when*. There's an assumption there that Jesus People will be a praying people. And the hallway of closed doors is the perfect place to go deep into the secret place of prayer.

Jesus didn't stop with "your Father who sees in secret." He added, "...will reward you."

We often imagine that reward means visible results—like the closed doors we've been staring at suddenly

---

126. Richard Wurmbrand, *In God's Underground* (London: Hodder & Stoughton, 1968), p. 135.
127. Ibid, 135.

swinging open into a new season. But the greatest reward of prayer behind closed doors isn't the change happening *around* us, it's what changes *within* us. Prayer purifies the motives of the heart. It loosens our grip on outcomes and strengthens our grip on God. It solidifies resolve, conforms us to the image of Christ, renews the mind, connects us to divine grace that sustains us in the waiting...and a thousand other graces desperately needed to live the Jesus way.

The closed door of the liminal season is God's invitation into a sacred space so easily overlooked. But the secret place isn't hidden because it's hard to find; it's hidden because so few go there.

We spend most of our lives trying to escape the very conditions that made Wurmbrand most alive to God. The majority of us will never endure the extreme captivity of a Romanian prison, but we will face our own closed doors. And like Wurmbrand, we'll have a choice when the doors stay shut: worship in the waiting and practice our righteousness in the secret place of thunder, or fight our way out.

The closed door is never an enemy, not when the One holding the key is the Father who sees in secret.

CHAPTER 12

WE SENSE WHAT HE IS ABOUT TO DO

"A message was revealed to Daniel. The message was true, but the appointed time was long."

- Daniel 10:1

The crowd at Tuks Stadium in Pretoria, South Africa, leaned forward, holding their collective breath.

It was April 2014. The event was the men's 100-meter final at the South African Athletics Championships, the most anticipated event of the meet. Among the sprinters stood a field of elite athletes, each one a mass of muscle and focus, crouched in their lanes like coiled springs.

"Ready."

The atmosphere crackled with tension. Years of training all led to this moment.

"Set."

The athletes rose into position; eyes forward, fingers pressed to the line. The starter raised his pistol.

Click.

No shot. No crack of sound. Just the *dink* of what sounded more like a toy gun.

Some runners, conditioned to move at the faintest cue, took off. Others hesitated, unsure whether to run or wait. It was chaos. Rhythms were broken. Momentum lost.

Officials called for a reset, but the damage had been done. What should have been the crowning moment of disciplined preparation unraveled into confusion, misfire, and frustration.

They had trusted that the signal to go would come with clarity.

It didn't.

This is what happens when you take off because you *think* you heard "Go," only to realize you moved without the authority of the one holding the gun.

Anyone who's ever stood in the space between seasons knows the temptation to take off at the faintest hint of "Go."

We've prayed. We've fasted. We've believed for breakthrough. And then we catch a glimpse of what God is preparing. That feeling of purpose begins to stir again. The air thickens with anticipation.

We sense just enough movement to make us think it's time to go…and we false start.

This chapter is about that tension. About resisting the urge to run ahead of God when we sense what He is about to do.

The Temptation to Get Ahead of God

One of the remarkable things about God is that He loves to reveal His plans. It's as if the joy of what's about to happen is too much to keep to Himself. Like a good Father whispering secrets to His children, He draws us close with hints and glimpses.

Amos tells us plainly,

> "Surely the Lord GOD does nothing unless He reveals His secret to His servants the prophets."[128]

And Jesus, pulling back the veil even further, said,

> "The mysteries of the kingdom of heaven have been given to you to know."[129]

God hides things *for* us, not *from* us. Like treasure in a field or pearls hidden in oysters, His revelations are concealed so that only the hungry will find them. As Paul writes,

> "What eye has not seen, nor ear heard, nor has entered into the heart of man...these things God

---

128. Amos 3:7
129. Matthew 13:11

> has prepared *for those who love Him*. But God has revealed them to us through His Spirit."[130]

There are revelations that God has reserved just for lovers. God isn't interested in satisfying casual curiosity. He hides His secrets to draw us closer.

> "It is the glory of God to conceal a matter, but the glory of kings is to search it out."[131]

When my kids ask me to play hide-and-seek, I don't hide so they can't find me. I leave clues to draw them to me. (Anyone else not want hide-and-seek to go on forever? Be honest.)

God is the same. He leaves hints about where He is, where He's going, and what's coming next.

But here's the tension.

Because the Spirit of God lives in us, because we are joined to Him in union, we begin to *feel* when He starts to move. Something deep within starts to stir. We can't always explain it. There's no "aha" moment to point to. But those who belong to Him sense a gentle nudge: the quiet whisper that the liminal season is drawing to a close.

It's in that moment when we face the greatest temptation—to run ahead of God.

It doesn't feel like rebellion.

---

130. 1 Corinthians 2:9–10
131. Proverbs 25:2

It feels like obedience.

Initiative.

Stewardship.

It feels like faith.

But it's not faith if it outruns God.

Because how can it be faith if it's rooted in assumption?

You say, "How is it assumption if He's the one showing it to me?"

Not every flutter of activity means *go*. Not every stirring means *now*. We can't mistake our sense of urgency for God's green light. There's an appointed time for every breakthrough. He is the One who determines times and seasons. The door to your next season belongs to Him.

It's like dinner at our house. Ok, not *exactly* like dinner at our house, but stay with me.

Lindsey is an incredible cook, and every night we're blessed by her gift. As she prepares dinner, the aroma fills the kitchen and spills into every room. And as that scent grows stronger, without fail, I find myself drifting toward the pantry…to "snack" while I wait.

But if I satisfy my hunger with pretzels, I dull my appetite for the main dish she's preparing. I settle for something inferior. I miss the fullness of what she intended to serve. All because I couldn't wait a few more minutes.

My appetite doesn't understand time. It only knows hunger. It smells food and it can't fathom waiting when satisfaction feels so close. This is where discipline has to tell the body that food *is* coming...and it *will* be worth the wait.

But the cook decides when it's time to eat,
not hunger.

That's what it's like when God begins to reveal what's next. The scent of what's ahead stirs desire. But if we're not careful, we'll reach for what's closest rather than wait for what's best.

Desire is a good sign, it means our hearts are alive to what God is doing. But desire isn't direction. The moment we move on impulse instead of the leading of the Lord, we drift from obedience. That's what happened to Moses.

When Moses Outran God

God had every intention of delivering His people from their bondage in Egypt. And by the time Moses arrived on the scene, the moment of deliverance was near. In fact, the Lord had already told Abraham what would happen generations earlier,

> "Know for certain that your descendants will be strangers in a land that is not theirs, where they will be enslaved and oppressed for four hundred years. But I will also judge the nation whom they

> will serve, and afterward they will come out with many possessions."[132]

What a fascinating word.

Strangers in a land? Check.

Enslaved and oppressed? Check.

Four hundred years? Hold that thought.

We don't know if Moses had access to this prophecy in the same way Daniel later studied Jeremiah's seventy-year promise.[133] But something in him sensed what God was cooking up. He could feel deliverance in the air. Freedom. Revolution. The pulse of heaven's timing drawing near for a people who had waited so long.

Stephen, recounting Israel's story generations later, tells us exactly what was burning in Moses' heart:

> "And he thought that his brothers understood that God was granting them deliverance through him."[134]

Moses was right about *what* God was doing, but wrong about *when*.

Being the born leader he was, when he saw an Egyptian beating a Hebrew slave, Moses snapped. Someone had to do something.

---

132. Genesis 15:13-14
133. See Daniel 9:2
134. Acts 7:25

So he did.

> "He looked this way and that, and when he saw no one, he killed the Egyptian and hid him in the sand."[135]

He looked this way and that…but never up. He thought the people were ready. He thought *he* was ready. But he never checked with the One holding the starter's gun.

Moses false-started.

And it cost him forty years on the backside of the desert.[136]

Remarking on how God dealt with Moses, Art Katz writes,

> "How many of us are itching to go out and make our mark for God? And yet God does not think it lavish, wasteful, or extravagant to give Moses another forty years of waiting in the wilderness until he is completely emptied out…The whole preliminary work of God is to disqualify us before we can be qualified. This is totally contrary to the whole religious mindset and spirit of the world, who would see this process as absolutely wasteful, because, after all, here is a man (Moses) who, at the age of forty, is full of vigor and ready to do great things for God."[137]

---

135. Exodus 2:12
136. See Acts 7:30
137. Katz, *Apostolic Foundations*, 14.

Moses may have been ready to do great things for God. He may even have rightly discerned what God was about to do for His people. But his timing was off....off by about ten years, actually.

Let's circle back to the four-hundred-year prophecy God gave Abraham.

God said Israel's bondage would last 400 years. But look at what Scripture records when the Exodus finally happens:

> "Now the time that the sons of Israel had lived in Egypt was 430 years. And at the end of 430 years, on this very day, all the multitudes of the LORD departed from the land of Egypt."[138]

The prophecy said 400. The reality was 430.

Let's do the math to see why reality didn't match the prophecy:

390 years – Israel's time in bondage when Moses begins his exile in the desert
\+ 40 years – Moses' exile

430 years – Israel's total time in bondage to Egypt

Moses' false start cost God's people an extra *thirty years* in bondage to Pharaoh.

Thirty more years of building bricks.

Thirty more years of mistreatment.

138. Exodus 12:40-41

Thirty fewer years of worshiping YHWH.

How many Hebrews died in Egypt during those extra three decades, never seeing the Red Sea split or hearing the Voice thunder from Sinai? How many were born in those thirty years who could have entered the promised land had they been born in the wilderness instead of captivity?

False starts have consequences.

Outrunning God isn't just costly for us, it delays deliverance for others.

Yes, God is sovereign. He causes all things to work together for good. Amen. But that doesn't mean we can force open doors He has kept shut and expect Him to clean up the wreckage. We must make room in our theology for human responsibility. God's people serving Pharaoh an extra thirty years was a direct result of impatience.

There is an appointed time for every breakthrough. Yes, waiting can feel like bondage. The liminal space can feel like building bricks: monotonous, exhausting, repetitive. One more day of doing the same nothing as the day before while wondering if deliverance will ever come. But we serve a God who *hears the groaning of His people and remembers His covenant with them*.[139]

---

139. Exodus 2:24

And when the fullness of time comes, salvation always wraps itself in flesh and comes to deliver.[140]

All our striving does is birth premature counterfeits.

For example, Saul was a counterfeit king, not an authentic representation of the way God ruled and reigned that would be seen in David. Ishmael was a half-son, not the covenant child God promised through Sarah.

Both stories began with people who sensed what God was going to do…but they just couldn't wait.

Rather than waiting for God to give them a king after His own heart, Israel made a demand and got Saul. Abraham believed God was going to give him a son, but when dinner took too long, He pulled Hagar into the pantry.

In each case, the seed was from God, but the timing was not.

The promise was pure, but the execution was carnal.

The outcome? Delay. Pain. Regret.

I can pick an apple off the tree in my backyard, but if it's not ripe, it'll taste bitter. But I can't blame the tree for bitterness when I picked the fruit too soon. The right fruit at the wrong time is still the wrong fruit.

---

140. Galatians 4:4

And God's promises can look ready before they're ripe. We must follow His leading and wait for His timing.[141]

God may show you what's ahead to call you out of the past, but that doesn't mean He's asking you to create the future.

He will birth Isaac, but only in His time.
He will deliver Israel, but not through murder.
He will establish David's throne, but only after Saul's legacy is removed.

Don't confuse revelation with permission. When the moment to move finally comes, you won't need to strive. The same Spirit who revealed what was coming will empower you to walk in it. And when you do, it will carry the unmistakable ease of grace. Until then, stay close. Keep listening. Let desire mature into dependence. And trust that when His whisper turns to command, you'll know—it's time.

---

141. The scope of this book won't allow me to do a deep-dive in how to discern the voice of God, but it's necessary to note here three principles that will help us discern the leading of the Lord: 1. Does it sound like Scripture, ie, something God would say? 2. Do you have people in your life—church leaders, someone discipling you, people you trust that have history with you and with God—who bear witness with what you believe God is speaking? 3. Have you taken time to pray through what you believe God is saying and given Him time to confirm it?

AN INTERLUDE BEFORE DOORS BEGIN TO OPEN

Beneath the surface of Psalm 25:12 is a beautiful image,

> "Who is the man that fears the LORD? Him shall He teach in the way He chooses."

The Hebrew word that we translate *teach* carries the image of an archer releasing an arrow. It literally means "to be sent out from the hand." Picture an archer with his bow drawn. The arrow rests at the corner of his mouth, so close it can feel the archer's breath. Before the shot is taken, there's a moment of nearness; intimate holding between archer and arrow.

That's what happens in the liminal space. God is near, fashioning you, aligning you, and drawing you so tenderly close. And at just the right moment, He releases you with accuracy and strength. As Eric Gilmour said,

> "His presence is better than a known path. It's better to recognize that God is with you than even knowing where God is taking you."[142]

The Whisper of Friendship

Psalm 25 continues the theme of intimate nearness that produces confident purpose,

> "The secret counsel of the LORD is with those who fear Him."[143]

The Hebrew word we translate as "secret counsel"—*sod*—is rich with imagery. It describes two people pressing closely together, sharing confidential things… the type of things that don't get said in public.

That's intimacy.

That's friendship.

That's God drawing you so close He can whisper what He's doing next.

Proverbs 3:32 echoes the imagery:

> "He is intimate with the upright."

Here, *intimate* paints a picture of trusted closeness, a fellowship of insiders who share the same heartbeat. It means a sense of covenantal one-ness that makes space for a confidential discussion.

---

142. Eric Gilmour, *His Presence is the Path,* Sonship International teaching, 2018.
143. Psalm 25:14

What's the implication?

God does not treat you as a stranger in the hallway. He is near. He is making space in the in-between for whispers to be heard about what's coming in the next season. Those whispers are vital. The confidential things He wants to share with you are essential for your next season. Don't miss them because you're too concerned with finding a way out.

Consider this: the season you're desperate to escape may be the very one God orchestrated to draw you near, and speak tenderly to your heart.

> "Behold, I will allure her, and bring her into the wilderness, and from that place I will speak tenderly to her heart."[144]

A Final Word for the Hallway

If you're in the liminal space right now, here's what you can trust:

> God is with you.
> God will lead you.

He's not pacing outside the door of your next season, anxious for you to find your way. He's standing with you in the hallway, whispering strength and strategy into your spirit.

And when the time comes;

---

144. Hosea 2:14

He'll pull back the string,
take His aim,
and send you out like an arrow.

Until then, trust the One who keeps every promise.

A Prayer for the Path Ahead

Father,
I trust You in the hallway.
Even when I don't know what's coming next,
I trust that You do.

Teach me to lean on You instead of my understanding.
Direct my steps, even when I can't feel them moving.
Give me ears to hear Your secret counsel
And a heart that trembles in joy at Your Word.

Aim me like an arrow.
Guide me like a friend.
Send me when You're ready.
And until then,
I choose to rest in Your presence.

Amen.

SECTION III

OPEN DOORS

THE THRESHOLD

Eventually, something shifts. The door opens. Or *many* do.

But the real test is knowing which one you're meant to walk through.

Not every open door is an invitation from God. Some are detours. Some are distractions. Some are good, but not right. That's why discernment matters so deeply in seasons of transition.

This section is about learning to recognize His voice more than just recognizing an opportunity. It's about moving forward with the same clarity and intimacy you learned in the hallway.

We don't move just because we can.

We move because we've been sent.

"I have put before you an open door which no one can shut."[145]

---

145. Revelation 3:8

CHAPTER 13

BEING SENT OR DECIDING TO GO

"If you don't have a word from God, you don't have any business going."

— Leonard Ravenhill

When Hudson Taylor stepped on the soil of inland China in the 19th century, he was entering hostile territory. The interior provinces were closed to foreigners, vehemently opposed to the gospel, and ripe with suspicion toward anyone who looked like him. Taylor knew the danger, but he also knew something far greater: he had been *sent* there.

On one occasion, a local magistrate stopped him at a crossroads and demanded to know who had given him permission to travel through the region. "You are not from here," the official said sharply. "You have no authority here." The path ahead seemed closed.

Taylor didn't argue. He simply reached into his coat and drew out a letter sealed by the British consulate. The royal crest gleamed in the light. The magistrate's tone changed instantly. What had been hostility turned into accommodation.

Taylor was a man under orders. He had been sent, and that made all the difference.

The Difference Between Going and Being Sent

When it's time to step out of the liminal space, there's a difference between deciding to go and being sent.

When we decide to go on our own, we go in our own strength. It's a movement of the will. It may be well-intentioned, but the source is wrong. And whether we realize it or not, we will carry the weight of that decision—the pressure to make it work, the fear of failure, the need to defend our choice.

But when we're sent, we carry something entirely different. We carry the authority of the One who commissioned us.

Like Hudson Taylor, the greater authority we carry opens doors and makes a way where there would otherwise be a dead end.

There are times in life when the closed door we've been staring at begins to open. In that moment, the most critical question isn't just *Am I ready to go*? The better question is: *Am I being sent*?

This chapter is about that distinction.

Because how we exit the hallway, and who sends us, will determine everything about what comes next.

Sent Ones in Scripture

In Luke 10, seventy of Jesus's followers return from their first mission trip, ecstatic. I imagine a noisy reunion: stories tumbling over each other, testimonies shouted across the room.

> "You should've seen it…he just got up
> and walked!"
> "I said, 'Come out in the name of Jesus!'
> and it did!"

The energy must have been electric. Jesus joins in the celebration, *"I saw Satan fall like lightning from heaven."* High fives all around. Then Jesus tells them how blessed they are to have seen and done what they just experienced.

All of this is found in Luke 10:17–18. But none of it happens without verse one:

> "The Lord appointed seventy others and
> *sent them…*"[146]

They didn't wake up one morning and decide to go do ministry. They didn't strategize, brand, and self-launch. They were *appointed*. Sent. They carried His name, His

---

146. Luke 10:1

message, His authority. The going was His idea, so what happened next was on Him.

That's why they could travel light. No money bag. No spare sandals. No suitcase full of resources. Just delegated authority and divine backing.[147]

Paul later called this posture *ambassadorship.*

> "We are ambassadors for Christ."[148]

Ambassadors don't speak for themselves. They represent the will and word of the one who sent them. Ambassadors don't improvise their message. They carry it. And ambassadors don't move under their own authority. They move under the authority of Another.

Israel's Return

There's a similar story in the Old Testament: the return of a remnant from Babylon to rebuild Jerusalem. Ezra tells the story of a monumental transition for God's people. But it says nothing about God's people waking up one day and thinking, "*We've been here long enough, let's get out of this hemmed-in bondage.*"

Quite the opposite.

Through the prophet Jeremiah, God told them to get comfortable in the liminal space. Though He knew the thoughts of peace He had for them, the door of that season wouldn't open for a while. Seventy years in fact.

147. Luke 10:4
148. 2 Corinthians 5:20

So go ahead, Israel, plant gardens and eat from them. Build houses and live in them.[149]

Then, when the appointed time arrived, God began to stir hearts in the kings who ruled over captive Israel. First, He stirred up the spirit of Cyrus, king of Persia.[150] Later, He stirred up Artaxerxes, another Persian king. This king was so moved with the purposes of God that he issued an official decree sending Ezra and a company of exiles back to Jerusalem to rebuild the temple and the walls.

The king even included a letter:

> "...you are being *sent* by the king and his seven counselors to inquire concerning Judah and Jerusalem with regard to the Law of your God which is in your hand."[151]

Ezra didn't initiate the journey. He didn't rally volunteers. He didn't organize a movement or fund a vision. He simply responded to the summons of heaven that had moved the heart of a king. He went out carrying royal backing and royal authority. If anyone questioned his mission, he could unfold the letter and point to the seal.

That's the difference between going and being sent.

If the king sends you, you're an ambassador.

If you send yourself, you're an explorer.

---

149. See Jeremiah 29:5, 10-11
150. Ezra 1:1
151. Ezra 7:14

The Power of Being Sent

It was January 14, 2025. I woke up to the Lord speaking about the difference between *going* and being *sent*.

The word was clear:

> "If you *go*, you go in your own authority. If you're *sent*, you're sent in the authority of the One who sends you."

This was a significant word for me because we were coming up on three years since moving to California. When we pulled into town on April 3, 2022, we arrived with vision and excitement for what God was going to do. We were certain God was about to explode the Central Coast with a glorious outpouring, and we had front row seats. Expectation was high. Revival seemed imminent.

Then one month turned to two. Two became four. And now we are counting our time here in years.

During these past three years, we've nearly run out of money more than once (I mean, can you even say you live in California if you haven't gone broke at least three or four times?). We've wanted to go back to the Middle East more than I care to admit, wondered if we missed God, and second-guessed our calling back to America. But every time we hit a wall, we turn toward heaven and remind God (and ourselves) that we didn't *come* here; we were *sent* here. And if God sent us, then *He's* responsible for the outcome. He determines the pace and tempo of what happens after the door opens.

That's the peace of being sent. It doesn't mean you avoid disappointment, or that things will move at the speed you want them to. But it does mean you can walk in the confidence of knowing the King sent you, and He always accomplishes His purposes through His faithful ones.

The burden to make something happen is lifted. You can walk in the peace that those walking in authority understand. Just look at the ministry of Jesus: He knew who He was, and He knew how He got here:

> "...the Father has sent Me."[152]

Jesus was the Father's ambassador. He didn't need to figure out what to do next. All He needed to do was keep looking to the One who sent Him and trust in His goodness... and then move forward in the authority of a Son sent on mission by His Father.

Look closer at what Jesus says in John 20:21. For context, this is after the resurrection. Having just passed through the closed doors His disciples were hiding behind, Jesus shows them His hands and His side. He then says,

> "Peace be with you. As the Father has sent Me, I also *send you*."

The same peace that Jesus experiences as the sent One of the Father, He extends to those He Himself sends under the authority of His name.

Closed doors won't hold Jesus back from coming and speaking peace to you. He wants to meet you in the

---

152. John 20:21

hemmed-in space between seasons and give you a fresh revelation of who He is. This will sustain you in your next season.

But we don't have to wait in that space in fear like the disciples did. We can confidently trust that Jesus will send us out of the hallway at just the right time with papers, authority, and purpose. The question isn't *if* the Lord will send us into our next season. The question is whether we'll be patient enough to wait on His timing.

Sent Ones Don't Just Do Something

This is why I disagree with the perspective of *just do something* and trust God to bless it. Sheep don't *just do something*. Sheep are led. They follow the Shepherd's voice. I want to know that the field I'm standing in, and the work I'm doing there, is under the covering of the Shepherd's will.

There's a saying I used to hear in the denomination I came up in: *I don't need a word, I've got a verse*. The point was we don't need to wait for a specific word from God before we move forward...we have the Great Commission. We've already been told to go and make disciples. Why wait when the command is clear?

It's well-intentioned. And it preaches great. But it's incomplete.

It doesn't reflect the fullness of how God leads His people.

Paul had the same verse we have (so to speak), yet even he waited until he was *sent.*

> "Set apart for Me Barnabas and Saul for the work to which I have called them."[153]

He knew his assignment wasn't general, it was specific. There was a particular people, in a particular place, where he carried particular authority.

> "...I have been made a minister to the Gentiles."[154]

Why did Peter stay among the Jews? Why did James remain in Jerusalem? Why did Philip find himself on a desert road with an Ethiopian official?

Because each one was sent—distinctly, deliberately, divinely.

The Spirit didn't just say, "Do *something.*"

He said, "Do *this.*"

And that makes all the difference.

I may not need Jesus to tell me where to have lunch today, but I *do* need Him to tell me where to plant my family. Where to give my life for the sake of the gospel. What door to walk through when there are dozens of good ones…and every one of them looks open.

---

153. Acts 13:1
154. Ephesians 3:8

The Trap of Need-Based Decisions

Let me paint a picture of what it's like to serve God at the crossroads of unimaginable *need* and unlimited gospel *opportunity*.

The gospel opportunity in an unreached region of the world like the Middle East is obvious. But when the opportunity to share Jesus with Muslims intersects with the tremendous needs caused by war, you find yourself standing in front of doors you never imagined.

This was the situation in Iraq from 2014-2018.

ISIS was ready to take over the world, and their base of operations was an hour down the road from us.

People were desperate to escape. The ones who were able to escape the grip of ISIS's rule in Mosul flooded into make-shift refugee camps. Thousands crammed into tent cities, living shoulder to shoulder in the desert. In addition to the basic needs of life, there were circumstantial needs—like women and children being protected from predatory men they were now living among. The most basic needs become logistical Jenga towers in the desert: people still need to get their hair cut, have access to medicine, and replace old sandals. Kids still need to play. The elderly still need to nap. Babies still need to be delivered.

The needs of a situation like this are unimaginable. Great, small, and everything in between.

So what do you do?

Well, brother, we preach the gospel to them. Jesus said make disciples!

Amen. Well said, smarty pants. But here's the problem; there are armed guards at the gate with orders not to let anyone in without the right papers. Yeah, that whole "letter from the king" thing isn't just a spiritual metaphor. Sometimes you need an actual letter from an actual authority saying you have actual permission to come in. And those letters aren't usually given to people who quote the Great Commission.

So how do you get in? How do you discern *which* crisis, *which* camp, *which* door?

That's the trap of need-based decisions.

There are a million and one needs in the world *right now*. And Jesus is the answer to every single one. While His resources are endless, mine are not. We are bound by time and space, finances and airplane tickets. So we have to ask: why this need? Why this door? Why this opportunity, and not another?

Why the feeding program for widows and orphans and not the barber shop ministry for young men in refugee camps? Why help the paralyzed from war when there are eight-year-old girls being sold to traffickers?

Need is a powerful motivator. But if need is what moves you, then need will also be what burns you out.

Because what happens when the need changes? What happens when the money runs out, or the visa expires, or persecution comes or the monotony of meeting that need year after year just gets...old? Or what if an opportunity comes to meet an even *greater* need?

If I made the decision to *just do something* because something just needed to be done, then my chances of just doing something *else* when something *else* needs to be done increases exponentially.

If I'm the one making the decisions about what doors I walk through, then I'm also the one in charge of which doors I close. What moves me through the door will also be the thing that eventually closes that door: my impulse. If it's me deciding to move into my next season, then it'll be me choosing how long I stay there.

That's how we end up bouncing from one good idea to the next, leaving behind a trail of half-built towers.

> "I gave them over to their own stubborn hearts, to walk in their own counsel."[155]

The world doesn't need more good ideas. The world doesn't need more good intentions. The world needs sent ones...men and women under authority, carrying the reality of Jesus wherever He assigns them.

If God is the One who moves me, then He's also the One who anchors me. He protects me from distractions. I don't have to worry about the flashy new opportunity. I don't have to worry about losing excitement when the honeymoon wears off. This is the joy of covenant. Saying

155. Psalm 81:12

yes to the Lord's leading means the freedom to say no to anything else that presents itself as an alternative.

God knows the needs that are around us. And He knows the people He is raising up to be the solution to those needs. But what *He* needs is obedient servants willing to do whatever *He* thinks is best.

You are formed and fashioned and gifted for a purpose. Don't dilute what God has formed in you by choosing to walk through any old door that presents itself as the most pressing need, or the greatest opportunity.

Need will always be the loudest voice in the room. Need will always beget need. We must be a mature people who trust God, obey God, wait on God, hear from God, and ultimately are sent out by God.

The Prayer That Sustains: God, You Said

Grab your highlighter. Here's the key to a powerful prayer life…

The three most powerful words you can ever pray are *God, You said*.

When things fall apart…

When the money runs out…

When the machete-wielding locals are running straight toward you, being able to turn towards heaven and say *God, You said* is like having a superpower.

When God sends you into the situation and everything in that situation goes sideways, the battle doesn't belong to you. It belongs to the One who sent you there.

Consider this: was Pharaoh Moses's problem or God's? How about Goliath; was he David's problem or God's? Sarah's barrenness, the walls of Jericho, the lion's den? None of those burdens belonged to the saints standing in front of them. And every one of them, in one way or another, stood before their problem and prayed a prayer that was as straightforward and history-making as *God, You said.*

God, this idea of delivering Your people from Pharaoh was *Your* idea.

God, this giant is lying about who *You* are.

God, *You* said Sarah would bear a son.

God, if these lions eat me then what does that say about *You*?

God, You said…and now this situation is trying to disagree with what You said. So what are we going to do about this, God?

But here's the thing about that stick-of-dynamite prayer: it's only legal to pray that prayer when I'm sent. If I move on my own, I forfeit the right to pray it.

I don't get to say *God, You said* if He didn't.

But if He did, and I'm sent into a situation that wars against the authority of the One who sent me, you better believe I'm looking to the King and confidently telling

Him the situation He sent me into is challenging *His* word. And God always defends what He commissioned.

The opposite of *God, You said,* is *what if?* And the same tongue can't speak both.

If God said, then there is no *what if.* There's only the certainty of knowing there is a letter in your pocket with the King's signature on it, declaring that nothing will stand in the way of what He sent you to do.

So if you hear nothing else in this chapter, hear this: Being able to cry out to God in your hardest moments, *God, You said,* is worth every second in the liminal space…a thousand times over. When the visa gets revoked, the enemy army rises against you, the disease refuses to leave, the prodigal won't come home, the house contract won't close, the product won't sell, the owner refuses to negotiate, and a host of other things that can happen in your next season…*God, You said,* is the most powerful, God exalting thing you could ever pray.

So wait for it.

Wait for the sending that gives those words their authority.

Following God's Timeline

Over the years, our family has learned to make significant decisions by asking one simple question: What is God saying? Not, *can we afford it*? Not, *is it safe*? Not, *does it make sense*? No. What is God saying?

Because if God is saying "x," then nothing will stand in the way of us walking in the authority, grace, and provision of God doing "x." If God is not saying "x" and we choose to move in that direction anyway, then we're choosing to move in our own authority, good intentions, and hope that we will be able to sustain ourselves in that direction.

We are so committed to this lifestyle of dependence on God that we've even prayed about the specific days He wants us to begin or leave a season. Let me give you two examples.

The First Flight

In late 2015, after we knew the Lord was sending us to Iraq, we began asking a very specific question: "When?" We were so ready to go. Week after week went by. Month after month. All of our stuff was sold, our bags were packed, the money was raised, but we still hadn't heard the *when*.

Then I had a dream.

In the dream, our family was at the airport. We were early for our flight. Waiting. Waiting. Waiting. Finally, an announcement came over the intercom. Our flight was boarding from Gate 411.

411...April 11.

With childlike faith, we determined April 11 was the day we were to begin our new season in Iraq.

<u>The Return Flight</u>

When our season in the Middle East came to a close, we approached it the same way: by seeking the Lord for His specific leading.

In early 2021, we knew God was leading us back to America. We just didn't know when. Then I had a dream.

In the dream, Lindsey and I were walking through the streets of her hometown. Friends came out to greet us, but we couldn't stop. As we walked away, we called over our shoulders, *"Don't worry, we'll be back in November."*

It seemed clear: we'd be leaving Iraq in November.

But as the months went by, we still had no details of *where* in America the Lord wanted us to land. We started to question whether leaving Iraq in November was the smart thing to do. Why leave where we are if we don't even know where we're going?

Then, in August, our oldest daughter, Layla, had a dream. In her dream, I was writing a check. The date on the check was simply the number *eleven*. When she asked why I was writing the check, I told her, "To protect my integrity."

Eleven. The eleventh month. November.

I wrote this in my journal:

> "This could mean we need to hold to November, even if it costs us something. We must protect

> our integrity before the Lord. Integrity means *the state of being whole* or *undivided*. We can't say, 'We'll move in November *if* God shows us where.' We must stand before Him with the assurance of what He's already spoken."

It also struck me that in the dream I was writing a check, not swiping a credit card. That meant the cost of obedience was real, but the resources were already in the account. We wouldn't need to borrow against something we didn't already have. God knew we had the faith to stand on and move forward with.

So on November 11, 2021, Lindsey and the kids said goodbye to Iraq and flew to stay with family in North Carolina. I followed ten days later.

We didn't know what was next. Only that God had said November.

We spent four months waiting in Lindsey's hometown, the same one from my dream, listening for what to do next. It was the journey of Abraham, who also left modern-day Iraq for a land the Lord would show him as he went.

And the same God who was faithful to lead Abraham also led us, but only after we obeyed what He had already said.

A Multi-Generational Lesson

This way of following God's leadership is something we've tried to model for our kids. And now that they're getting older, they're doing what they've seen us do so many times.

When Layla was deciding whether to attend Bible school after graduating from high school, she earnestly sought the Lord for His leadership. She fasted. She prayed. She waited. She determined she wouldn't move forward until she heard from God. No matter what her desire for the next season was, no matter the opportunity, no matter the need of beginning her own life and ministry, Layla was not going to move herself out of the hallway.

After weeks of seeking the Lord, the *day before* her deposit for school was due, He spoke. I won't go into detail, it's too sacred for me to share. The point is: she refused to move into her next season without being sent. And the Lord honored that by speaking so clearly to her about where He wanted to send her.

Then came the question of how to pay the $8,000 tuition bill.

How much do you think Layla worried about that?

Not. One. Bit.

That's the power of *God, You said*. When you have that prayer because you have His promise, things like tuition bills aren't addressed to you. They're sent to God's mailbox.

As I write this, Layla isn't stepping into her next season because she made a well-informed decision after asking dozens of people for their opinions. She's being sent with the blessing, authority, grace, and provision of God. She's not just going to Bible school. She's on assignment from heaven, born from the secret place of thunder. She's got papers from the King. When things get hard, she won't quit because she knows she would be quitting on God. When other opportunities present themselves, she won't be distracted by them. No matter what this next season holds for her, she has *God, You said* on her lips.

This is the way of those who walk with God. Jesus People don't chase opportunity, they follow the leading of the Lord. They don't make good decision, they obey. They don't respond to need or opportunity, they respond to the Voice.

The world is filled with good ideas, noble intentions, and pressing demands. But only those who are sent carry the authority of heaven.

When the storm hits, when the way gets hard, or when the next door looks too good to pass up, the question that steadies the heart is: *Did God say*? If He did, then stay your course. Carry your papers. And when difficulties come, drop to your knees and pray the three words that have shifted history and shaken empires: *God, You said*.

Oh, and about Layla's $8,000 tuition bill? The Lord spoke to a precious family and asked them to cover the *entire amount*.

That's what being sent looks like.

CHAPTER 14

THE TEST OF MULTIPLE DOORS

"The secret counsel of the Lord is for those who fear Him."

- Psalm 25:14

Our family was in Istanbul for a short stay. At that time, our daughter Adalei was around 9 years old. We had booked two adjoining rooms—Lindsey and I in one, the kids in the other—connected by an interior door that created one big space. We were all exhausted from the travel and fell asleep pretty hard.

At some point in the night, the phone next to our bed rang.

"Hello?"

"Mr. Broere?"

"Yes."

"We have your daughter."

I can't think of many things more terrifying to wake up to at 2 a.m. in a hotel in Istanbul.

Thankfully, it wasn't the Turkish mob, it was the front desk.

Adalei had woken up disoriented. She tried to come into our room but, half asleep, walked out the *front* door instead. Once she was in the hallway, she couldn't remember which door led back to our room.

So she wandered through the hallway, knocking on random doors, until a kind man (an angel?) walked out, realized what was happening, and brought her down to the lobby. She was able to tell them who she was, who her parents were, and the staff found our room in the system.

Crisis averted.

But the image stuck with me: a long hallway, multiple doors, and no clear idea which one is the right one.

This chapter is about that space; when you're not sure which way is the right way. When multiple doors appear at once and you're left asking, "Which door is God's door?"

The Test of Many Doors

We often think of waiting seasons as ones where every door seems closed. But sometimes the test isn't the absence of options, it's the abundance of them.

Which job? Which city? Which ministry path? Which school?

It can feel like God handed you a ring of keys but didn't label the locks.

But God isn't a game show host waiting to see if we'll pick the correct mystery door. He's a Father, always inviting us deeper into the place of nearness.

The answer of which door to walk through is never an issue of us making the right choice. It's in us continuing to prioritize intimacy with the God of all doors.

Intimacy is the Key

God promises in Psalm 32:8,

> "I will instruct you and teach you in the way you should go; I will guide you with My loving eye upon you."

What a word. What an anchor of hope. I can't tell you how many times that passage has steadied my heart in the bewilderment of transition and reminded me that God Himself is committed to leading His people.

Years ago, I was in the Congo during a significant season of transition. We knew the Lord was calling us into a new ministry opportunity, but we didn't know much more than that. In fact, there were multiple doors in front of us, and all of them opened up to great ministry opportunities.

On that trip to the Congo, I had brought a copy of *Secrets of the Secret Place* by Bob Sorge. In it, Bob highlights the promise of Psalm 32—but he also points out a warning:

> "Don't be like the horse or the mule, which have no understanding, which must be harnessed with bit and bridle, else they will not come near you."[156]

Sorge points out the key phrase: "Else they will not come near you."[157]

That's the issue, isn't it? Nearness. Proximity. Intimacy.

Horses and mules, by nature, are not going to come close to the rider. They will constantly wander off on their own path of impulse. By doing this, they become unfruitful. So the rider must harness the animal so it can be led where the rider wants to go. But the Lord doesn't want to lead us that way. He wants us to draw near to Him, and from that place of intimacy, He can lead us like lovers… with just a glance.

> "Some people are mulish. They just don't get it. They pull away from their very source of life and care and feeding. It hasn't penetrated their thick skulls that the smartest place in the universe to be—and to stay—is right next to God...the wisest thing you'll ever do in this life is draw close to God and seek Him with all your heart."[158]

---

156. Psalm 32:9
157. Bob Sorge, *Secrets of the Secret Place* (Oasis House, Greenwood, Missouri. 2001), Pg. 31
158. Ibid, 32.

When we're in a season of transition, we can become so focused on which door to choose that we forget who's holding the keys. We stare at the options instead of the One who opens and shuts them. The key to the right door is always cut and polished in intimacy with Jesus.

When Layla was praying about whether she was to attend the Bible school I mentioned earlier, she had an encounter that helped keep her focus right. As she prayed and waited on the Lord, she saw His hand on the handle of a closed door. She strained to see what was behind it. Was the door going to open to Bible school? Maybe a different path?

The Lord gently lifted her chin until all she could see was His face.

A week later, she had her answer; not because she figured out what was behind the door, but because she focused on the One who stood before it. It was intimacy with the God of all doors that unlocked her next season.

Sorge continues,

> "When you pursue this intimacy, you will begin to unlock the greatest secrets in life. It's here He guides you with His eye and directs your heart with His heart. Sometimes we tend to make life decisions based upon our appraisal of surrounding circumstances and conditions. However, the Lord doesn't want us getting our direction from looking outward but from looking upward. He wants us receiving life direction by

> beholding His beauty...and then being guided by the gaze of His eye."[159]

After two decades of marriage, Lindsey can say a thousand things to me with a single glance. Marriage is designed to mirror our relationship with Jesus, which tells me there's a level of communication between us and God that transcends words. Burning bushes and angelic visitation are exciting, but if I still need those things to know what He's saying, that's an announcement I haven't yet cultivated the kind of intimacy with Him that can lead with just a look.

> "Intimacy precedes insight. Passion precedes purpose...God doesn't simply want to get you on the right path, He wants to enjoy you throughout the journey. He doesn't want you to find His will and then take off running. God's primary desire for your life is not that you discover His will and walk in it; His primary desire is that you draw near to Him and come to know Him. And then from that knowing relationship there comes a tender walking together in His purposes."[160]

I couldn't have said it any better.

Thought Worms

A 2020 neuroscience study from Queen's University found that we have about 6,200 thoughts per day, and the thought rate spikes during moments of decision-

---

159. Ibid, 32.
160. Ibid, 32.

making. Researchers called the transitions between thoughts *"thought worms."*[161]

When we're in the hallway between seasons, those thought worms multiply.

What if I make the wrong choice?

What if I already missed God?

What if years are wasted in my indecision?

I'm a certified expert in the "*what if*" spiral. Through my own extensive study and field research, I've concluded that imagination, left untended, becomes a runaway train 100% of the time.

The result? I'm no longer listening for God's voice. I'm just arguing with myself in the dark.

Not only does this pull us away from intimacy with Jesus, it also robs us of rest. We start worrying about things that may not even be true, imagining scenarios we can't control. None of those "thought worms" are fruitful. We become like the mule from Psalm 32, driven by impulse rather than led by intimacy.

But if we can silence that internal dialogue and return our focus to Jesus, not only will we know the direction He intends us to move in, but our joy will increase dramatically.

---

161. *New study suggests we have 6,200 thoughts every day* - Big Think (https://bigthink.com/neuropsych/how-many-thoughts-per-day/?utm_source=chatgpt.com.

When Joshua was leading God's people into the Promised Land, the Lord told him exactly what to focus on:

> "This Book of the Law shall not depart from your mouth, but you shall meditate on it day and night... for then you will make your way prosperous, and then you will have success."[162]

God didn't tell this new leader to analyze military strategy and memorize all seven habits of highly effective people. He said, "*Focus on me.*"

Your problems aren't really your problems, they belong to Jesus...as long as you keep your eyes on Him. But when you start giving unnecessary attention to the things happening around you, you take ownership of those situations. We are designed to meditate on Him and His word, not our circumstances.

This is the same language that opens the book of Psalms,

> "Blessed is the man who walks not in the counsel of the ungodly...but his delight is in the law of the Lord, and in His law he meditates day and night...whatever he does prospers"[163]

When the mind starts spiraling, peace doesn't come from trying harder to figure things out. It comes from

162. Joshua 1:8
163. Psalm 1:1-3

returning to stillness and intimacy with Jesus; where His voice is clear, His Word steady, and His presence near.

When a Door Is a Test

Sometimes God opens a door because He intends for us to walk through it. Other times, He opens a door to see if we trust Him enough *not* to. The door becomes a test to see if we're ready to handle the next season.

You might think, "*That's awful, God would never do that.*" Perhaps you're getting *testing* confused with *tempting*. James 1:13 tells us God will never tempt us. But make no mistake, He does test us. For example, the entire wilderness experience for Israel was a test:

> "Remember that the LORD your God led you all the way these forty years in the wilderness, to humble you and *test* you, to know what was in your heart, whether you would keep His commandments or not."[164]

Even feeding the 5,000 involved a test. When Jesus asked Philip where they should buy bread for the crowd,

> "He said this to *test* him, for He Himself knew what He would do."[165]

David also lived in this tension. When Saul hunted him through the wilderness, there were multiple open

164. Deuteronomy 8:2
165. John 6:6

doors for David to walk through that would have eliminated the threat and seated him on the throne.

When Saul walked into the cave where David and his men were hiding, who opened that door?

When David and Abishai found Saul sleeping in his camp with his spear beside his head, who set that scene?

That's a trick question. If you've made it this far into the book, you already know: *all doors belong to God.*

Abishai correctly discerned who was opening the door, but he failed the test:

> "Then Abishai said to David, '*God has delivered your enemy into your hand this day*. Now therefore, please, let me strike him at once with the spear, right to the earth; and I will not have to strike him a second time!'"[166]

But David refused to walk through that door.

> "As the LORD lives, the LORD shall strike him, or his day shall come to die, or he shall go out to battle and perish. The LORD forbid that I should stretch out my hand against the LORD's anointed."[167]

God had opened a door that David was never meant to walk through. David had to be tested: Would he

166. 1 Samuel 26:8
167. 1 Samuel 26:10-11

walk in the ways of God's kingdom, trusting the Lord's timing? Or would he follow the world's wisdom, grabbing what seemed like divine opportunity?

As I once heard, "Some doors are opened just to see whether or not we will embrace the inferior."

When multiple doors appear, it's not time to make good decisions, it's time to draw near. God's not just trying to get you to the right decision. More than anything else, He is always leading you to *Himself*. The answer to what we should do next is always found *in Him*.

> "In Christ are hidden all the treasures of wisdom and knowledge."[168]

He wants to show you the way with a glance, not a pointed finger.

The Test of Multiple Doors

If I were a betting man, I'd be willing to bet the farm on this: when God begins to move you out of the liminal space and into your next season, there will be no shortage of opportunities suddenly presenting themselves. I've seen it too many times to count. In fact, I was talking with someone just *yesterday* about this very thing happening to him.

Recently, the Lord spoke to his wife about him going to ministry school. It felt eerily similar to when the Lord directed me into that kind of season.

168. Colossians 2:3

In addition to having a shepherd's heart for God's people, my friend also has a passion for cooking. He's dreamed for years of owning a food truck. And wouldn't you know it, just two weeks after the Lord stirred his wife to pray about ministry school, someone reached out to him with a "once-in-a-lifetime" opportunity to relocate his family to a place with half the cost of living and takeover a…wait for it…food truck business.

What are the odds?

I'll tell you what the odds are: 100%.

When God begins to shift your season, the test of the liminal space isn't over, it just changes shape. Suddenly doors of opportunity are popping open all around you. Which is why it becomes all the more vital to stay close to the One who's leading you, so you can discern which door is *His.*

And right about now, I can almost hear you asking, "Well, that's great, Neil…but how do I know which door is God's door?"

You'll know.

Seriously, you'll know.

> "My sheep hear My voice, and I know them, and they follow Me."[169]

169. John 10:27

Does a sheep worry about finding its way to the next pasture? Of course not. Leading is the shepherd's responsibility. Staying close is the sheep's.

I was once in a field outside Bethlehem, marveling at the beauty of the countryside surrounding Jerusalem. In the distance, I heard an odd chirping sound echoing through the valley. Curious, I walked toward it and discovered an old man leading a flock of sheep. Every few minutes, he let out the distinctive chirp to keep his sheep on track.

As long as the sheep were in earshot of the shepherd's voice, they were safe. When one drifted too far, he would move closer to draw them back in. While they focused on eating, he focused on them. They were so confident in their shepherd, so comfortable in his presence, that they could simply do what they were designed to do in the place their shepherd had them.

"My sheep hear My voice…and they follow Me."

It's no coincidence that Jesus tells us He is our Good Shepherd right on the heels of saying He's also the door.[170] Just saying.

Just like those sheep in the fields of Bethlehem, there will be an internal knowing when the Shepherd is leading you into a new field. There will be a settled peace inside responding to the Voice telling you, "This is the way, walk in it."[171] I'm not saying there won't be questions or

---

170. John 10:9
171. Isaiah 30:21

hesitations about how it's going to work. But deep down, you'll know which door is God's door.

And as you continue to follow the Good Shepherd, you'll start recognizing His voice more quickly. You'll realize that the random dream wasn't so random. That sense you had deep in your gut wasn't just the pizza. That stirring in your spirit as you read that verse? It wasn't just emotionalism.

The longer you follow the Shepherd, the more you'll discover He's really good at speaking your language… and leading you on His paths.

Over time, and through the changing of seasons, you'll build a kind of spiritual muscle memory of how to handle the test of multiple doors. Like David, you'll grow confident enough to recognize when a door looks right but isn't *yours.*

A Final Thought

The shepherd's chirp isn't reserved for the special sheep. The counsel of the Lord isn't hidden among the gifted and anointed. It's for those who are intimate with Him, or as the Bible often says, those who fear Him.

> "The secret counsel of the Lord is for those who fear Him."[172]

His counsel isn't secret because He's hiding it from us. It's secret only because so few come close enough to find it. He hides His treasures in the light of His presence. It's

172. Psalm 25:14

only when we stay at a distance that we end up fumbling in the dark for door handles.

And His tests? They're always open-book. *Do not let this Book depart from you day or night.*[173]

173. Joshua 1:8

CHAPTER 15

TODAY IS THE LANGUAGE OF GOD

"The opportunity of a lifetime must be seized in the lifetime of the opportunity."

- Leonard Ravenhill

On July 16, 1969, at precisely 9:32 a.m. Eastern Time, a rocket weighing over six million pounds lifted off from Launch Complex 39A at the Kennedy Space Center in Florida. Inside were three men—Neil Armstrong, Buzz Aldrin, and Michael Collins—squeezed into the cramped cockpit of the Apollo 11 spacecraft. Their destination: the moon.

What most people watching that day didn't realize was how fragile the window of opportunity really was. NASA had calculated a narrow "launch window," only a few minutes wide, in which the rocket could depart and still intercept the moon's orbit 240,000 miles away. A delay of even ten minutes would mean missing the target entirely. The next viable window would be weeks away, and even then, the alignment of orbital mechanics, fuel load, and mission logistics would need to be recalculated from scratch.

Inside Mission Control, engineers and flight directors were tense. Any number of issues like weather, instrument malfunction, human error, could have forced a hold. But at 9:32 a.m., everything fell into place. The skies cleared. The countdown reached zero. And the door opened.

Three days later, Neil Armstrong became the first human to set foot on the lunar surface.

But it was the narrow door that opened on launch day that made history possible.

There comes a moment in every liminal season when the door opens. But those doors don't remain open forever. As we've seen, the next season can be forfeited by not waiting well in the hallway. It can also be missed by not moving when God says go.

Lot's Last Morning in Sodom

Lot knew something about doors and shifting seasons. He had traveled with Abraham in his B.C. days (extra credit if you caught that), journeyed to the Promised Land God spoke so highly of (even though it looked more like a barren desert), took a detour with Abraham down to Egypt, and *finally* settled in his own space. After all the wandering, all the waiting, Lot finally found his dream home in the booming metropolis of...Sodom.

What's not to love about the city that has it all?

But when two angels showed up at the city gate, Lot must have known something was off. And these guys weren't playing around. Perhaps it was the way the men of the city greeted them, or maybe they were just uptight angels. But whatever the case, they weren't there to negotiate. They had come for Lot.

The door of escape had opened, but it wouldn't stay open for long.

Lot welcomed the messengers into his home, completely unaware that the final countdown for his city had already begun. Sodom had crossed a line with God, and what came next was no longer a matter of *if*, but *when*.

> "We will destroy this place, because the outcry against them has grown great before the face of the Lord."[174]

But Lot hesitated.

Even after the warning. Even after the mob at his door the night before.

Maybe it was the familiarity. Perhaps it was fear. Maybe he just needed more information before taking action. Scripture doesn't give us his reasons, only his reaction.

> "But he lingered."[175]

---

174. Genesis 19:13
175. Genesis 19:16

So the angels took him by the hand—him, his wife, and his two daughters—and physically pulled them out of the city.

> "The Lord being merciful to him, and they brought him out and set him outside the city."[176]

Lot had to be dragged through the door that God had mercifully opened for his deliverance. He wasn't rebellious. He just flinched. And that hesitation nearly cost him everything.

And even then, the instructions were crystal clear: *Do not look back. Do not stop. Escape to the hills.*

A certain sobriety was required to walk through that door. Forward movement was paramount. There could be no looking back.

But forward was not the direction Lot's wife was willing to go. Something in her heart was still tethered to the past. Wicked or not, Sodom was home. It was comfortable. Familiar. What lay ahead was unknown. In that decisive moment, moving forward seemed careless. *Can't we think about this some more? How do we know this is the right thing to do? We don't even know where God is taking us.*

So she looked back. And in looking back, she removed herself from the protection that obedience would have provided.

---

176. Genesis 19:16

> "But his wife looked back behind him, and she became a pillar of salt."[177]

By morning, the city was gone. Fire fell from heaven. Smoke rose from the valley. The door was closed, and the opportunity was over.

Here's the takeaway: there's a difference between patiently waiting on God and delaying obedience when He opens a door. One is faith. The other is fear dressed up as discernment.

Mature saints learn the difference.

There are *seasons* of patiently waiting in the liminal space, and there are *moments* of obediently moving forward.

Seasons prepare you.

Moments propel you.

That's the challenge. It's hard to go from a standstill to a sprint. But when God says *move*, there is a grace available to move. And that grace isn't waiting for you to feel ready. It's not pausing long enough for every question to be answered. Grace moves when God moves.

We can't put off to tomorrow what God is asking us to do today.

---

177. Genesis 19:26

Today, If You Hear His Voice...

The writer of Hebrews recalls how Israel's unbelief kept them from entering God's promise. He was leading them through the transition of being slaves in Egypt to sons and daughters in a land of promise. But they couldn't make the shift. And their failure becomes our warning:

> "Today, if you will hear His voice, do not harden your hearts as in the rebellion...I swore in My wrath 'They shall not enter My rest.'"[178]

There is a sacred moment called today that's designated for announcing the open door of God's will. There is a grace present in *that* day to hear the instructions: *this is the way, walk in it.* There is a divine push present there to move you in the direction of the Lord's leading.

Today. Not tomorrow.

Andrew Murray put it this way: "Today is the language of the Holy Spirit, tomorrow is the language of the tempter."[179]

Wow.

Today speaks the language of faith. Tomorrow whispers the tongue of unbelief. Don't think to yourself, "That word is too big for today, it needs to wait until tomorrow; the demand of that word is too great for today; maybe tomorrow that word will be easier."

---

178. Hebrews 3: 7, 8
179. Andrew Murray, The Holiest of All: An Exposition of the Epistle to the Hebrews (1894), 123.

> "Do not say I will do this tomorrow, you don't know what tomorrow will bring."[180]

Delay in believing today what God says He can do will always harden your heart tomorrow. That was Israel's story.

The believer who answers the *"Today"* of God's word with the *"Tomorrow"* of a more favorable situation unknowingly creates an unsuitable environment for the word. By delaying what God is giving you the grace to do today, you are choosing to walk by sight and not by faith. This has the detrimental effect of hardening your heart towards God's word. The environment of faith is where the seed of His word comes alive.

Consider the parable of the sower in Matthew 13. The same seed that fell on good soil and produced an increase also fell on hard soil and never came alive. Same seed. Different result. The issue is never the word sown; it's the environment that receives it.

The seed of God's word won't penetrate the soil that has become hard. Delaying until tomorrow what God is sowing today has the same effect on the soil of our hearts.

I've seen this scenario play out many times: someone has the call of God on their life. He hems them in to prepare them for the next season and form the necessary character that can bear the weight of what He wants to do next. But they get stuck on the launch pad.

---

180. James 4:13

Maybe it's a job that keeps them from moving forward.

Maybe a new romance feels too fragile to leave.

Maybe it's fear masquerading as "wait for confirmation."

I've seen numerous "good" things hamstring those called and commissioned from moving forward when the door opens. The hallway becomes comfortable, and what was meant to be transition becomes home.

I'll never forget the first time God gave me a prophetic picture for someone as I prayed for them. Let's call her Melissa. As I prayed for Melissa, I saw a picture of a sailboat with its sail raised high. But instead of catching wind on the open sea, it sat motionless in the harbor. I knew the sailboat was designed to be out at sea, but there it sat, ready but still.

When I shared what I saw, Melissa laughed nervously. She told me the Lord had called her to the mission field. She even knew the exact place He was sending her. But she delayed. She got a job at a ministry school, helped out at church, and got comfortable in the in-between.

As far as I know, she never left the harbor.

Lord, Let Me First...

When we're hemmed in between seasons, it can feel like the most important thing is just getting out of the hallway and into what's next. Yet when the door finally opens, something in us still hesitates. The irony of it all.

> "Then He said to another, 'Follow Me.' But he said, 'Lord, *let me first* go and bury my father.'...And another also said, 'Lord, I will follow You, but *let me first* go and bid them farewell who are at my house.'"[181]

What's your *Lord, let me first...*? Is it a family situation like the man who wanted to first bury his father?

What's interesting about that story is the bigger issue wasn't a funeral, it was finances. In that culture, a son couldn't claim his father's inheritance unless he was present for the burial. The hesitation to follow Jesus wasn't love for family so much as it was financial security. He wanted a backup plan in case the door Jesus was opening didn't work out.

Or perhaps your *Lord, let me first,* is similar to the man who wanted to turn and say goodbye first? But that's Lot's wife all over again, tethered to what God had already called her to leave behind.

> "No one, having put his hand to the plow, and looking back, is fit for the kingdom of God."[182]

Don't wait for more suitable conditions tomorrow. Don't wait for strength and courage to build, hoping that

---

181. Luke 9:59, 61
182. Luke 9:62

obedience will be easier tomorrow. Don't wait for your feelings to change so the sacrifice will be less painful tomorrow.

Hear the word of *today* and receive it by faith with an obedient *yes.*

> "Do not worry about tomorrow, what you will eat, what you will drink, what you will wear...seek first the kingdom of God (*today*)."[183]

Burn the Ships

There's a story about the Spanish conquistador Hernán Cortés that illustrates this point perfectly.

In the spring of 1519, Cortés arrived on the eastern shore of Mexico with eleven ships, six hundred men, and an impossible mission. The Spanish crown had sent him to explore, claim new territory, make alliances, and, though unstated, secure wealth. But what lay ahead was the Aztec empire: powerful, vast, and far greater in number than his small band of soldiers.

The odds were stacked against him. The terrain was unfamiliar. And his men were restless.

Whispers of mutiny made their way through the ranks.

The ships they arrived in were anchored just off the coast; visible, tangible reminders that retreat was still an option. If things went south, they could always go home. The ships represented safety, escape, plan B.

183. Matthew 6:33

Cortés made a decision.

He ordered the ships to be burned.

The message was unmistakable: *We're not going back.* The only way out is through.

It was an irreversible act. Bold. Ruthless. Final.

With the ships gone, his men were no longer explorers, they were settlers. Stakeholders in whatever came next. With no way back, they were forced into full commitment. And in time, against all odds, they would succeed in taking the Aztec capital.

Sometimes we have to burn the ships. There comes a point when prayer must turn into action, when we put feet to our faith and move forward.

Like the Lord told Moses on the shore of the Red Sea:

> "Why do you cry out to Me? Tell the children of Israel to move forward."[184]

You can't stay in the prayer meeting forever. At some point, the fast ends, the sea parts, and the first step has to be taken.

> "And truly if they had called to mind the country from which they had come out, they would have had opportunity to return."[185]

---

184. Genesis 14:15
185. Hebrews 11:15

Paul told the church in Corinth that a "great and effective door has opened to me, and there are many adversaries."[186] Does that mean he froze in fear and prioritized personal safety with clever decision-making strategies? Of course not. Recognizing the opportunity for the gospel to be spread in Ephesus, Paul walked through the door and remained a gospel witness in that city for three years...*in spite of the adversaries.*

That's what it means to seize the opportunity of today.

Every open door carries this invitation: to trust that God has timed it perfectly, even when you don't feel ready, even when the way forward looks impossible.

The hallway teaches us how to wait, but there comes a moment when it's time to move. And that moment rarely comes with all the answers. But it does come with grace to obey...and grace to go.

The Midnight Door

It was December 1851. Harriet Tubman stood just outside Dorchester County, Maryland, cloaked by winter darkness and pine trees.

Behind her, a small group of fugitives trembled. Several had never stepped beyond the boundaries of the plantation. One woman held her child so tightly the child had gone limp in her arms. They were free in theory, but

186. 1 Corinthians 16:9

not yet in reality. The door had opened, but they hadn't walked through it.

Behind them, slave catchers were closing in. A notice had gone out just days earlier in the *Cambridge Democrat:* "$100 reward for each person returned, $1,200 if the entire group was recovered alive."

The Fugitive Slave Act of 1850 had made every inch of American soil dangerous. Even in free states, no one was truly safe. Anyone could be seized and sent back South. There would be no safety until they crossed the Canadian border, hundreds of miles away.

Tubman, just twenty-nine, had escaped slavery herself two years earlier. Now she risked everything leading others to freedom. She would eventually make thirteen trips south, guiding over seventy people to freedom.

She was a woman of grit and strategy. But the key to Tubman's success was her *timing*.

That night, the Wicomico River lay ahead. By morning, the tide would rise, and the trail they now stood on would be swallowed up. Behind them were bounty hunters, bloodhounds, and the threat of death.

But in that narrow window, between midnight and dawn, a path stood open.

Tubman turned to the group and whispered the only words that mattered: "*We go now.*"

No time for debate. No room for hesitation. A single delay could cost them everything.

And though they didn't know what lay ahead, they knew the door was open. But only for a moment. Deliverance was possible, but only for those bold enough to step into it by faith.

Remember Lots Wife

The hallway was never intended to be home. It was the crucible where God forged something in you. The waiting, the wrestling, the weeping…it all had a purpose. But even preparation has an expiration date.

Not everyone makes it out of the hallway. Some are lulled to sleep by stillness. Others are paralyzed by what might lie beyond the door. But the liminal space is not the land of promise; it's the space *between* what was and what will be, between what God did and what He's about to do.

God doesn't intend for the liminal space to last forever. Don't let it.

Remember Lot's wife.

Step through the door.

Burn the ships.

Don't look back.

Trust that your time in the hallway accomplished its purpose. Believe that God faithfully formed in you what was essential for what's next. And now that season is upon you. Walk forward with confidence, even if you don't have the clarity you hoped for. What matters at this moment isn't understanding. It's obedience.

But that's a different book.

EPILOGUE

There's a large field around the corner from our house. When we first moved in two years ago, the field was full of wildflowers and herbs. But somewhere around the time I began writing this book, large machinery was brought in. A massive undertaking was clearly underway. I wondered if the property had been sold to developers.

Come to find out, the owners of the field had decided to grow strawberries.

During the majority of the time it took to write this book, that field was undergoing a season of preparation; transitioning from being a place of wild growth to a well-ordered, intentional operation designed to produce fruit.

When I drove by the field this morning, it was a frenzy of activity—dozens of workers picking ripe strawberries, big yellow tractors running the rows with boxes full of packed fruit, 18-wheelers headed for the distribution plant where the strawberries would be shipped all over the country. Signs of life and progress were suddenly everywhere.

But the "suddenly" of all that activity didn't come with a snap of the fingers. It was preceded by a long, slow season of preparation. The plowing and shaping was indispensable. The waiting was costly but worth it. Now the same land that brought the owners no profit in a previous season has become an asset for the family for generations.

Watching that transformation unfold in real time has been a living metaphor for the message of this book. And as we move out of our own in-between and take our seat in the dawn of a new season, it's time to take everything God formed in the quiet corridors of the hallway and let it become fuel for the road ahead.

Few things compare to the confidence of knowing you are precisely where God intends you to be. And as we've learned, whatever this new season holds—success or sorrow, fruitfulness or famine—we're ready. We are prepared. We've been sent here by the King Himself. Come what may, we have God, and that's enough. We carry the assurance of those who have walked with Him through the in-between.

And when the time comes to stand in the liminal space again, we'll stand with muscle memory. We'll recognize the feel of the hallway beneath our feet, the familiar decor of trust and surrender, perhaps even glimpse our own portrait on the wall—proof that we've been there before. We'll move with the steady grace of those who have learned to trust the unseen hand that guides them through the transition.

We never walk those halls alone. So as you encounter others in their own in-between spaces, share with them what you've learned. Tell them of the God who meets us there. Offer them what the Lord offered you: trust, patience, and hope.

Until we meet again, great grace upon you in your new season. May the God of all peace strengthen you. May your days be marked by the love of Christ, the fellowship of the Holy Spirit, and the confidence of one who knows they are a child of God.

Grace and peace,

NEIL

NEIL BROERE is a writer, teacher, and pastor known for his insights into God's word, kingdom, and church. He serves as teaching pastor at Radiant Central Coast in Grover Beach, California. Driven by a passion for the gospel to spread like wildfire across the earth, Neil also serves as the Global Director of Becoming Love Ministries, where he pioneers new gospel initiatives around the globe. Neil and his family served as missionaries in Iraq for 6 years before moving to California in 2022. When Neil is home on the Central Coast of California, you'll find him surfing, riding around in his old pickup, and enjoying the outdoors with his family.

Neil is also the author of ***Obedience, Suffering, & Reward:*** *Discovering God's Redemptive Beauty in the Struggle*

For more information about Neil, please visit www.NeilBroere.com

Sign up for Neil's weekly devotional email, *Between Sundays*, at www.NeilBroere.com/ Between-Sundays

For more information about bulk ordering
this title or other works by Neil Broere,
contact the publisher at:

Tall Pine Books
PO Bo 42 Warsaw, IN 46581
www.TallPineBooks.com

www.ingramcontent.com/pod-product-compliance
Lightning Source LLC
LaVergne TN
LVHW091119080826
845145LV00008B/1974

* 9 7 8 1 9 6 7 2 6 2 3 8 0 *